The White Use
of Blacks
in America

Books by Dan Lacy

THE WHITE USE OF BLACKS IN AMERICA
THE MEANING OF THE AMERICAN REVOLUTION
FREEDOM AND COMMUNICATIONS

The White Use of Blacks in America

350 years of law and violence,
attitudes and etiquette,
politics and change

Dan Lacy

McGraw-Hill Book Company

New York • St. Louis • San Francisco • London • Düsseldorf

Kuala Lumpur • Mexico • Montreal • Panama • São Paulo

Sydney • Toronto • Johannesburg • New Delhi • Singapore

Designed by Kathleen Carey
Reprinted by arrangement with Atheneum Publishers

Library of Congress catalog card number: 77-175286

First McGraw-Hill Paperback Edition, 1973

07-035751-X

1 2 3 4 5 6 7 8 9 MU MU 7 9 8 7 6 5 4 3

*This book reflects something of what I learned
about human beings, black and white, from*

TOLBERT HARDY LACY

1877–1943

to whose memory it is dedicated

Preface

The last decade has seen an outpouring of books about race problems in America. Many of them have been hasty compilations or popularizations seeking to capitalize on a hungry and sometimes uncritical library market, stimulated in turn by federal appropriations and by new programs of black studies. Others have been sincere polemics reflecting an opened black militance or a revived white concern. Serious scholarship ripens more slowly, but there has been a steady growth in competent and objective research as well.

The post–World War II years have brought important revisions in our understanding, for example, of slavery, of Reconstruction, of African backgrounds, and of the social psychology of race. But especially important has been the flood of new writing about black history and the black community itself, most of it by black writers. This greatly neglected aspect of American history has been remarkably illuminated not only by historians but also by sociologists, anthropologists, and social psychologists. Black novelists, poets, dramatists, and essayists have also made a special and unique contribution to the understanding of black history.

Though the dynamics of that history arise primarily within the black community, which will increasingly shape its own future, most problems that blacks have confronted have been created by whites. Most studies of white actions and attitudes toward blacks in America have treated them as the product of irrational racist emotion and as problems in social psychopathology. Though there has been a marked paranoid component in white racial attitudes, white actions with regard to blacks have not in fact been an aggregation of irrationalities. In their totality they have constituted a deliberate and carefully interlinked set of policies intended to assure the presence and the exploitability of a large semiskilled labor force, primarily in agriculture, whose labor could be commanded at subsistence rates. Changes in the economy that increased or diminished the need for such a labor force have been the principal determinants of racial policy. Indeed, the paranoid elements in American, and especially in Southern, racial attitudes have been in no small part deliberately cultivated as a means of sustaining racial policies having primarily economic objectives.

This book tries to do something somewhat different. It is not, except incidentally, about black history; it is about these questions of white policy. I am myself a white man, a Southerner, and what I have been trying to understand and to recount here are the economic, political, social, and personal policies of my fellow whites and the causes and the consequences of our actions. I hope it will help us, through seeing patterns of the past, to shape those of the future.

PREFACE

Every book is engendered and nourished by more men and women than can be named in an acknowledgment. The dedication is to my father, who was a lawyer in a North Carolina black-belt town. Forty years ago, more than twenty years before the Supreme Court decision against school segregation, I had expressed to him some smugly liberal pride that the town had just built a Negro high school, a newer and better building than the white high school from which I had recently graduated. "Yes," he said, "I guess it's nice; but I can't help wondering what kind of Americans they'll have a chance to grow up to be, going off to school by themselves that way." The statement startled me, for no other arrangement had ever occurred to me as possible and I had never before heard anyone refer to Negroes as "Americans." By one path and another, that casual remark and the way of thinking it revealed led ultimately to this book.

There is a more immediate debt to Thomas J. Wilson, old friend and fellow North Carolinian, long the greatly distinguished director of the Harvard University Press. In his tragically brief time at Atheneum, after he retired from Harvard, he had suggested the book and had very helpfully reviewed the first few chapters before his death. Had he lived, it would have been a kind of joint venture. In a way, it still is.

June 1971   DAN LACY

Contents

xi

The White Use
of Blacks
in America

Introduction

No white man is happy with the situation of blacks in America. There are some who believe that the relative poverty, ignorance, and spiritual exile in which far too many blacks live is a national disgrace and an indictment of American society. But the unhappiness of most is more ambivalent. They denounce blacks as lazy and lacking in ambition while they resent black competition for jobs. They are angered by taxation for relief payments to unemployed Negroes and equally angered by the admission of Negroes to employment formerly reserved for whites. They are disgusted by evidences of black ignorance and resentful of black demands for improved and integrated schools. They are contemptuous of the filth of ghetto slums and fearful of black intrusion into white suburbs. They ridicule black irresponsibility and fear black assertions of responsibility. They resent the burden on white earnings and the threats to white equanimity imposed by the isolation and poverty of blacks, and even more they resent efforts to achieve the integration and the effective black participation in society that would end those burdens and threats.

3

And yet whites must face the fact that the situation of blacks in America is no accident. The presence here of more than twenty million Negroes, their social, economic, and educational state, indeed the whole condition of their lives, have been in large part determined by deliberate white policy. For more than three centuries it suited the ends of white America to have at its command a large semiskilled labor force, compelled to work for a bare subsistence. For the feudal landlords and the early industrialists of Europe economic necessity provided such a labor force. Landless peasants worked to the landlords' terms or came starving to the city to accept any employment the factory owner offered. But to assemble and hold such a body of laborers in a continent where the open land offered itself to every taker and where every tradition spoke of the freedom and equality of all men required extraordinary measures.

To meet what the dominant whites thought were their needs, they had to create a labor force that was not free to share in the abundance of land or compete for the skilled jobs opening in industry, that did not share in the Declaration's equality of all men or participate in the Address's government by the people, that was denied that determination of one's own destiny that America meant to its other children. To achieve this goal required a vigorous and coherent public policy made up of laws, of folkways, of diligently implanted attitudes. It required the participation of the state, the churches, the schools, the press, and society generally. Yet for all its complexity and difficulty, such a policy was executed with remarkable effectiveness and with all but complete success. The smooth collaboration of governmental, institu-

4

tional, and private action is without parallel in our history. We assembled and maintained that labor force—large, productive, and consuming only at the margins of subsistence—through all the kaleidoscopic changes of our history: through the colonial period, through revolution and independence, through the tidal sweep to the Pacific, through the Civil War and Reconstruction, through the creation of the vast cities and overwhelming industries of modern America.

In the last generation our goals have changed. The mindless machine can do the work of the unskilled, and the landowners once desperately dependent on black labor now turn from it in indifference. The unskilled or semiskilled labor force that was once a necessity is now an embarrassment, unusable in our economy. The lack of training for more skilled or professional occupations, once deliberately designed to hold blacks in low-paid jobs by barring them from competitive attractions, is now exceedingly costly. The white community is faced with providing a minimal support for the unusable portion of the black community and with the fears and uncomfortable embarrassment arising from the poverty and disorder in the urban slums in which the workers displaced from agriculture have been segregated.

It suits us, therefore, now to reverse our policies and quickly to transform the black labor force into a skilled one, capable of self-supporting integration into our modern technological economy. The new policy is, however, a halting one and inconsistently pursued. Though it has the impassioned support of those relatively small groups in the white community who had denounced our earlier policies as unjust, it still meets with sullen opposition from those determined to avoid the competition of skilled black labor and from those moved by irrational waves of racial fear and hatred. For it was a cunning and necessary part of the general white strategy of exploiting blacks to create among whites a profound revulsion against blacks as such. In no other way could general white support or at least acquiescence have been won for policies and programs that often damaged the interests of poor whites as well as blacks and that offended every American precept of equality and liberty. The disfranchisement of blacks, their exclusion from equal educational and occupational opportunity, their residential and social segregation, the violence perpetrated on them by the forces of law and lawlessness alike—not to mention slavery itself—could never have been enforced without implanting deeply in the subrational emotions of whites the conviction that blacks were a different and inferior group of beings, to be rejected and feared as well as used by the white community.

We live now with this inheritance of fear and aversion, which stands ominously in the way of all the measures required to reintegrate the black labor force into the economy at a new and productive level and to eliminate the other problems and embarrassments presented to the white community by the alienation and poverty of so large a part of the black.

The policy we now seek to follow is represented by such measures as the Job Corps, the Community Action Programs of the Office of Economic Opportunity, the funding of special education programs in areas of poverty, efforts at educational integration, and the special recruiting and training programs of corporations. But, hampered by ambivalence and halfheartedly pursued, this policy has faltered from the beginning. Discouraged that this weak program has not in a few years undone the results of three centuries of a vigorously pursued opposing policy, we are tempted to abandon even our small efforts and to resign ourselves to drift.

But this will not work either. The continued presence in the society of an alienated community of millions not equipped to participate effectively in the economy will present intolerable problems. If we can no longer use in our economy a distinct caste of serfs, we have no choice but to pursue a policy of full economic integration of the black community, with all its implications of political and educational integration as well.

And since, if we are to avoid chaos, our new policies must achieve their results in a fraction of the time we devoted to those policies whose results we must now efface, they must be pursued with at least as total and comprehensive a devotion. To make blacks equal contributors to the economy, equal sharers of its benefits, and equal participants in the government of the people by the people will require as thorough and dedicated a union of public and private efforts as we formerly devoted to excluding blacks from those aspects of equality.

But another dimension has been added to the problem. Hitherto the destiny of blacks in America has been determined largely by the policies of whites. Blacks were brought to America because whites needed them to work the tobacco and rice and indigo and later the cotton fields. They were enslaved by whites because their masters found them easier to control and more profitable as slaves than as indentured servants. They were kept illiterate by white design, subdued by white violence, apprehended in their escapes by white law. They were partly emancipated in 1865 by uneasy white consciences but kept in a state of semiservitude by a new set of white devices. White decisions determined thereafter how much and what kind of education there would be for blacks. White-made laws enforced segregation in public accommodations; white real-estate policy determined where blacks could live; decisions by white employers and white labor unions determined what jobs they could hold. Whites determined whether and where blacks could vote.

But that is changing. By slow determination and sacrifice and by using white consciences, the black community has accumulated substantial economic and educational resources. It has come to share in some, if as yet small, degree in political power. It has been able to recall the Constitution to life to protect its rights. In a country in which nine-tenths of the people are white and more than nineteen-twentieths of the economic resources are white-owned, black policy must always find its way through white realities. But black power to help determine the future of the black community may achieve what the newer and divided white policies could not achieve alone. If so, black power will have been the means of saving our national community as the fit residence of the society we have dreamed of and of restoring to us our role as a nation conceived in liberty and dedicated to the proposition that all men are created equal.

CHAPTER ONE

In Which Free Land Enslaves Blacks

THE LAND STRETCHED away endlessly from Jamestown, up the broad river, blue then between its wooded banks, past the falls and hills of the Piedmont, past the ranging mountains no white man would climb for a century yet to come, past unimagined distances beyond, in which all Europe could disappear. North and south lay an empty coast from the French hamlets on the frozen St. Lawrence to the palm-shaded Spanish settlements of Florida. There was land beyond all dreams, beyond all belief—land enough for every serf and peasant of Europe to build his home, land enough for bold men to carve out lordly domains, land enough to destroy the meaning of a feudal system based on a monopoly of the soil.

That abundance was to be America's greatest blessing. Land was plentiful; men were scarce. Land, because of its very abundance, lost the power through which its owners were able to assert lordship over the peasants of Europe and dominate the society and governments of that continent. Men, because they were so few in the American wilderness, were to achieve an individual worth they had never known before. More than the Declaration of Independence or the Constitution or the Bill of Rights, more than the words and labors of a Washington or a Jefferson or a Lincoln, it was the land that gave men liberty.

But ambitious men were thwarted by this very abundance. Of what good were domains of thousands of acres if a man could make actual use of only those he could clear and plant with his own hands? And how could an owner get men to work his fields for him if every laborer could go out to the frontier of settlement and take land for himself? During the early decades of colonization, the vision, the energy, and the funds for organizing the settlement of America came from such aggressive men— not from landless peasants seeking a freehold for themselves in the New World but from adventurers seeking wealth.

Before men could make their fortunes in the western wilderness two things were needed. Some commodity had to be found for which Europe had an avid demand, that could be mined or grown in the new settlements, that could survive the long voyage to market, and that was worth enough to pay exorbitant freight costs. And a labor force had to be organized that would work very cheaply and that could be held to its tasks in the face of the mighty temptation of the empty oceans of land opening to the west.

The Spanish and Portuguese settlers, who had been in the New World for more than a century before the coming of the English to Jamestown, had found their solu-

CHAPTER ONE

tions to both these problems. The gold and silver mines of Mexico and Peru, the sugar plantations of Brazil and the Caribbean islands, and, on a smaller scale, the cultivation of tobacco and indigo provided the wealth-giving staples. Aztecs and tribes of the Inca empire, skilled in the extraction and working of metals and already disciplined to labor for their native rulers, provided a ready force for the mines.

For agricultural labor, the Spaniards and Portuguese turned to African Negroes, with whom they had become familiar as a result of the Portuguese exploration of the African west coast in the fifteenth century. Some thousands of African slaves were indeed employed in Spain and Portugal even before the first settlements in the New World. The sugar plantations of Brazil and the Caribbean islands were manned almost from the beginning by blacks, and slavery was a well-established institution throughout Hispanic America long before the first English settlement at Jamestown. When the British came to occupy Barbados and Jamaica, the techniques of growing cane and making sugar, the use of a Negro labor force, and the patterns of a slave-based plantation economy were soon copied, obliterating the yeoman society that had first been established.

Frost was sugar's enemy, and the cane could not be grown in the latitude of the English mainland settlements. But the organizers of the first colonies had another New World staple in mind as well: tobacco. This seductive weed had been widely known to the Indians before the first white settlement and was introduced throughout Europe in the sixteenth century. It had already rivaled or surpassed sugar in importance in many of the Caribbean islands and was a major crop in Brazil when John Rolfe introduced its culture to Virginia in 1612. Quickly its cultivation became the dominant economic activity in Maryland and Virginia, the one hope of the settlers to create a prospering economy. Initially prices were very high, and a fever of tobacco-planting absorbed the Chesapeake colonies throughout the seventeenth century.

The crop produced a high return, but it required a great deal of labor. Plants had to be started in seed beds, tenderly transplanted to carefully prepared fields, thoroughly and frequently cultivated, and picked, cured, and packed with skill. Moreover, tobacco quickly exhausted the fertility of soils and required a constant clearing of new fields. The tantalizing opportunity of wealth that lay before the first settlers could be realized only if they could command a considerable number of workers who could bear these burdens. But labor could not be hired, at least not for wages a planter could afford to pay without losing his golden profits. It was too easy for the worker to clear his own land and work for his own wealth rather than for another's.

To the tobacco planters of Maryland and Virginia as to the mine owners and sugar planters to the south, unfree labor seemed the only answer. Even New Englanders felt the same economic pressures. It was Emanuel Downing, a Massachusetts man urging a war against the Narragansett Indians in 1641, who stated the argument for all colonists hungry to grow rich from exploiting the abundance before them: "If upon a just warre the Lord should deliver them into our hands, we might easily have men, women, and children enough to exchange for

Moores [by which he meant Negroes], which will be more gaynful pilladge for us than wee conceive, for I doe not see how wee can thrive until wee get into a stock of slaves sufficient to doe all our buisiness, for our children's children will hardly see this great continent filled with people, soe that ourr servants will still desire freedome to plant for themselves, and not stay but for verie great wages. And I suppose you know verie well how we shall mayntayne 20 Moores cheaper than one Englishe servant." (Massachusetts Historical Society *Collections*, XXXVI, p. 65, as quoted in Ulrich Bonnell Phillips, *American Negro Slavery*, p. 101.)

Though Negroes, in some form of servitude, were present in Virginia at least as early as 1619, it was to their fellow whites that enterprising colonists first turned as a source of unfree labor. There were many reasons for this. Tobacco, unlike such later staples as rice and indigo, required skilled individual work rather than gang labor. Farm laborers from England could fit more easily into the small-farm economy of seventeenth-century Maryland and Virginia than could African blacks speaking strange tongues and untrained in Western agriculture. This was even more true of the cereal agriculture, the fisheries, and the handicraft and commercial economies of the Northern colonies. English workers were only too ready to migrate from a country torn by civil war for much of the century. The same domestic turmoil had prevented England's entering the slave trade on a large scale, and the Portuguese and Spanish ships that might have supplied the English colonies with blacks were barred from their ports. Even if there had been practicable channels of trade, the struggling English colonists could not have bid successfully for slaves against the planters of the Caribbean islands and the Latin American mainland. Nor, until the idea was imported from Jamaica and Barbados, did the mainland English have any experience with or precedent for chattel slavery.

The indentured servitude of whites was a different matter, however. The voyage to America and the achievement of a foothold on that strange continent was a difficult and expensive barrier. Thousands of Britons, and later Germans, longed to go but did not have the cost of passage or the means or experience to establish themselves in the New World. For them, an arrangement that would provide for their transport, that would assure them of food, clothing, shelter and training while they adjusted to the new environment, and that would later give them land and tools was a profitable one. There was no lack of willing men and women ready to indenture their service for a term of years to gain these benefits. A legal pattern was ready to hand in the English system of apprenticeship under which youths were indentured to work for masters for a term of years, trading their labor for sustenance, training, and a start in life. Colonial legislation gave a further stimulus by a system of headrights that gave to every landowner another fifty acres for each indentured servant he brought over.

Hence it was that throughout the seventeenth century the labor of clearing and planting the British colonies of North America was generally performed by English laborers brought to America under indentures that obliged them to work for a master for from four to seven years in exchange for passage money, training, and sustenance. Probably two-thirds of all the migrants to North America during the colonial period came as indentured servants.

But indentured servitude did not solve the needs of the Southern colonists. Their lands remained hungry for labor. As more of the forests were cleared away, as capital accumulated, as systems of factors and bills of exchange matured, and as available ocean transportation increased, the small Southern farms grew into commercial plantations. Large gangs of workers were needed who could be held to hard, routine, disciplined labor. Especially was this true as rice and indigo culture was established in the lower South. These crops could be economically grown only on a large scale, with abundant labor available for the various stages of their complex cycle of growth and processing.

Even more importantly, the free land to the west called ever more temptingly to the white worker. Indistinguishable from his white fellows who were freemen, the indentured servant could readily escape to the frontier, where he was almost certain to avoid detection. The demand for servants was so great and their flight so easy that to hold them it was necessary to reduce the term of service, lighten the burdens, and increase the benefits of the indenture. Yet every concession that made indentured servitude more tolerable to the servant made it less attractive to the master. To operate profitably the large tobacco and rice plantations that were coming into being by the end of the seventeenth century, ambitious men needed a permanent and involuntary labor force whom they did not need to induce to sign an indenture or to cajole to remain at their task, who did not need to be replaced every few years with new hands, and who could be whipped to their labors.

The seventeenth century was not tender of human life or human freedom. Children could be hanged for stealing a penny or starve in the gutters of London or Paris if they could not buy or beg their bread. But the time had passed when the conscience of white men would let other white men be bought and sold or chained and whipped at the will of a master. (Writers of the time usually said it was "Christians" who could not be so treated, but they meant "white men." Jewish, Muslim, or atheist white men were not enslaved in the seventeenth century, but black Christians were.) In the conscience of the times there was little to protect a black who, though he might doubtfully be conceded to be a member of the human race in a biological sense, was not a member of the human society within which there were bonds, however slender, of brotherhood and mutual respect.

Hence by the eighteenth century the American settlers, and especially the Southern planters, turned, as had their Caribbean and Brazilian predecessors, to the enslaved African as the basis of their labor force. They were the more able to do so because the economy of Western Europe and the colonies had become large enough to sustain a massive transatlantic trade in which blacks were systematically seized in Africa and transported in an enormous and regular flow to the New World as the principal payment for its sugar, tobacco, rice, indigo, naval stores, and precious metals. England herself had moved from a marginal to a principal supplier of slaves, so that the North American colonies now had access to the traffic. By the mid-eighteenth century they had themselves become active participants in it, so that it was likely to be Massachusetts or Rhode Island slavers who delivered the cargoes to Norfolk or Charleston or Savannah.

No censuses were taken in the colonial period, and our estimates of the black population of the colonies, both free and slave, are but guesses. But a good guess is that by 1700 there were 30,000 Negroes in the mainland English colonies. By 1750 this figure had probably risen to 250,000. On the eve of the Revolution there was a black population of half a million, of whom all but a tiny minority were slaves.

More significant than their numbers was their role in American society. The considerable number of blacks in the Northern colonies were for the most part household servants, and with some exceptions they played a marginal and relatively unimportant part in the economy of the region. But in the Southern colonies the situation was quite different. By the late colonial period the economy of those commonwealths had been built around the production and export of staple crops. These were produced on large commercial plantations, which could function successfully only on the basis of large, permanent, disciplined labor forces. Small farms devoted to subsistence agriculture of course existed in large numbers in the South and indeed probably absorbed the labor of a majority of the white population. But this type of farming could prosper only in areas remote from water transportation where a commercial plantation producing for export would be at a competitive disadvantage. Hence the subsistence economy in the South was dominant only in North Carolina, an almost land-locked colony, and in the hills and back country of the other colonies.

Fatefully, the Southern economy had been firmly rooted in a type of production that required a labor force that could not be made up of free men. Once Southern society became organized in this way, it became stable and rigid, and only a cataclysm could reorient its economy in ways that would not require the use of an unfree and hence black labor force.

In this the Southern English colonies were not peculiar. A plantation or mining economy in which nonwhite slaves labored under duress to produce minerals or agricultural staples for export to Europe was the characteristic pattern of European exploitation of the New World. The later dominance of the free white society of the Northern United States and Canada has blinded us to the basic reality of the colonial period. And this is that slavery was not a dark and alien exception to the New World's freedom but was rather the basic instrument by which Europe mastered the Americas and sought to wring wealth from them. In the seventeenth and eighteenth centuries far more blacks than whites were brought to the New World, and from Chesapeake Bay to the Rio de la Plata the economic life of the Americas was built on slavery. Even in New England and the Middle Colonies, where slavery had only a marginal existence, the colonists made their living indirectly from the slave economy, supplying flour, fish, breadstuffs, barrel staves, and shipping services to the Southern and West Indian settlements and engaging themselves as principals in the slave trade.

In European tradition and learning there remained

memories of Roman chattel slavery and of medieval villeinage and serfdom, but in Northern and Western Europe and especially in Britain the law by 1600 had come to presume the personal freedom of all men. It was necessary hence to create a new kind of social arrangement, based on a new legal code. This necessity was confronted first in the West Indies. In consequence the legal and institutional patterns of slavery on the mainland were copied from those of the British islands of the Caribbean, especially from those of Barbados, and these in turn from earlier Spanish and Portuguese models. Prior to 1700 there was little systematic legislation on the mainland dealing with slavery. Such acts as there were related for the most part to the recovery and punishment of runaway slaves. They make it clear, however, that slavery was a well-established and fully recognized institution long before there was legislation formally defining the status of slaves.

Probably in the seventeenth century most of the colonists thought of slavery in terms of indentured servitude, differing from the servitude of whites in that it was involuntary, permanent, and hereditary. But what a difference! However harsh the concept of indentured servitude, its hardships in practice were alleviated by the necessity of offering terms that would entice settlers to indenture themselves, by the need to hold workers whose escape was easy, and by the community sense of what was fit treatment for fellow whites. None of these protections availed the black; and, perhaps reinforced by Spanish precedents, it was the Roman legal concepts of chattel slavery that ultimately defined the American institution.

As in Roman law, the slave codes enacted in the

Southern colonies in the eighteenth century conceived the slave as a *res*, a thing, whose person as well as whose labor was owned by a master. Whatever the personal relationship in individual cases, the legal relationship of the master to his slaves was much more nearly that of an owner to his cattle than that of an employer to his employees. Slaves could be bought, sold, bequeathed, inherited, mortgaged, or seized for debt like any other property. They and their children forever belonged to the master. They had no civil status before the law; they could not own property, or marry, or make contracts, or sue or be sued, or testify in most cases, or serve on juries. They had no political status; they could not vote or hold office or acquire citizenship, nor did they enjoy the protection of the common law. Though the wanton or deliberate killing of a slave was murder, he had no protection against the assaults of his master, and whipping was a recognized and customary form of punishment and training. The master was, indeed, held guiltless even of the death of his slave if it was the unintended consequence of punishment.

The slave codes in fact were intended not to protect slaves from the harshness of masters but rather to protect the community from their leniency. The codes were replete with provisions against the education of Negroes, their assembly in meetings, their having access to arms, their being permitted to leave their place of employment without written permission, and against any other liberty that might permit them to plot insurrection. As slavery became a fixed institution and as blacks came greatly to outnumber whites in the principal plantation areas, the fear of black revolts became a haunting and painful anxiety never absent from Southern thoughts. To break the individual independence of blacks and to prevent their uniting to reassert it became a central necessity for the preservation of slavery and the command of unpaid labor.

By 1750 the legal structure of slavery was substantially complete. In the mid-nineteenth century, when the slave system reached its full maturity, the slave codes were to be revised into a more consistent and comprehensive whole. But this revision would add nothing to the fundamental legal concepts that were developed in the colonial period. All that slavery was to become in the United States was fully implied in the institution as it existed in 1750.

The terms of the great paradox at the heart of American life had been set. The mass of the people of Europe had been the landless dependents of the lords of the soil; the endless lands of the Western world offered them freedom and independence. The primitive innocence of the New World contrasted with the corruption of the Old and offered the hope of a New Jerusalem, a land called to be an example of purity and freedom. Yet the very value the New World set upon men and their labor led to slavery. The very freedom of some men to go out and work for themselves rather than for a master demanded an end to freedom for others. The legal bonds of slavery replaced the economic bonds of feudalism, and every clause of the slave codes was an equipoise to the frontier's freedom. The very abundance that liberated and enriched the white men who came to America was the cause of the enslaving of the black men who were brought here. The economy of the New World through whose open doors the European migrants came to seek their fortune was founded, directly or indirectly, on the labor of slaves; and the building of the pure temple of freedom in the New World was made possible only by the revival of an institution of naked tyranny foresworn for centuries in the Old.

But the white men had solved their immediate problem. They had found the means to exploit the New World's treasures, to clear the fields and grow the staples Europe and Britain hungered for, and to maintain on the edge of the frontier's anarchy an organized labor force that could be compelled to work for bare subsistence in the midst of plenty.

CHAPTER TWO

In Which the Declaration That All Men Are Created Equal Makes Blacks Not Men

BY THE LATE eighteenth century the use of slaves had become much less profitable. The thin soils of the Tidewater counties of Virginia and Maryland had been leached out by the pounding Southern rains and the exhausting tobacco culture. The growth of staple crops for export was not practicable on the new lands being opened to the west, remote as they were from navigable streams and usable roads. A chronic overproduction of tobacco had depressed prices. Yet no corresponding reduction of costs seemed possible to planters who owned large numbers of slaves that must be at least minimally fed and clothed and housed, whether or not they could be profitably employed, and who themselves were committed to a semifeudal pattern of life involving heavy annual expenditure. The remorseless increase of debt that followed added spiraling interest charges to their burdens.

The mounting financial despair of the planters of the South was no doubt a spur to revolution and helped to account for the fact that in that region—in contrast to the Northern and Middle colonies—men of wealth solidly supported the secession from the Empire. Men like the master of Mount Vernon turned for their principal staple from tobacco to wheat, a crop ill adapted to gang labor, and from farming to Western land speculation as their chief hope of gain. They denounced a system of slavery that shackled the master to his servants and bound up his capital in a labor force that could not be efficiently used. They counted the gains that might be theirs if the money tied up in slaves could be invested instead in Western lands. The active British encouragement of the slave trade throughout the eighteenth century, which had been so eagerly welcomed by the planters at an earlier day, now became a ground of complaint against the British Crown.

The profitability of slavery received further sharp blows from the Revolution itself. The export of tobacco was almost entirely stopped in the war years; and when it was resumed with the coming of peace, the Americans no longer had an assured monopoly of the British market. With the end of British bounties, the naval-stores industry waned and the culture of indigo collapsed. The export of rice to the West Indies was nearly closed off during the war. In the latter years of the conflict the British occupation of Southern ports and key inland points and the bitter fighting throughout the region further disrupted the plantation economy.

The relative unprofitability of slavery in the Revolutionary era opened the ears even of slaveholders to the voices of those who thought it was not only unproductive but wrong. All during the colonial period there had been consciences made uncomfortable by the buying and selling of men. But blacks had profited little from this sensitivity. Puritan and Catholic divines alike had been able to find Biblical and theological justification for an institution that had become so indispensable to the economies not only of the New World but of the European motherlands themselves. By 1760 a third of the entire British merchant fleet was engaged in the slave trade, bringing 50,000 or more captives a year from Africa to the New World, and the African suppliers of slaves absorbed a large part of British industrial output in exchange. The colonial products most advantageous to the Empire were produced by slave labor, and even the products of free labor in the Middle and Northern colonies found their markets principally in the Southern and Caribbean slave economies. This dependence was even more true of the Spanish and Portuguese empires. It is little wonder that moral justification was so readily found for an institution that appeared so useful. Indeed, whatever moral concern existed with respect to slavery in the colonial period was almost never directed against the institution itself. Rather it was directed toward mitigating specific aspects of slavery, such as cruel punishment or the separation of families, toward offering opportunities to slaves for religious instruction and conversion, or toward opposing the enslaving of Indians. Indeed the protectors of Indians at times actually welcomed the importation of Negro slaves as a morally preferable alternative.

But the question of conscience became more troublesome with the coming of the Revolution. The colonists had based their early protests on the ground that the British government had acted in ways that contravened the specific provisions of colonial charters or the fundamental rights of British subjects. But when they had seceded from the Empire, abrogating their charters and renouncing their loyalty to the Crown, these arguments lost their validity. The Americans were compelled to seek a broader justification of their Revolution, one resting on the rights of all men rather than on those of Englishmen. They found this justification in a fundamental concept of the British seventeenth-century revolutions—a concept derived ultimately from Christian beliefs. And that is the concept of the fundamental equality of men. The entire philosophy of the Revolution was based on the statement which Jefferson and the signers of the Declaration of Independence believed to be a self-evident truth: that all men are created equal.

Such a statement was in obvious and irreconcilable conflict with a system in which some men could be owned by other men. The conflict bit the deeper when the declarers of independence went on to say that liberty was one of the unalienable rights to which their equal creation entitled all men. But the contradiction was not only between the formal statements of the Declaration and the formal provisions of the slave codes. The conflict was rising in the hearts and emotions of men. The Declaration of Independence and the Bills of Rights of the Revolutionary state constitutions said what they did about equality and liberty because there was in fact a genuine upwelling of belief in those ideals. Slavery came to offend not only the logical minds but the more generous emotions of the Revolutionary generation. And as the institution seemed to be less and less useful to the economy and particularly to the large owners of slaves, conscience had a wider scope and a more receptive audience than it would otherwise have been permitted.

Antislavery sentiments had not, in fact, been unknown in the century before the Revolution. Quakers in particular had become increasingly concerned about their own relationship to slavery, especially after the re-examination of the Quaker role in public affairs that came with the French and Indian War. Quaker meetings, though not yet demanding the end of slavery or even the immediate emancipation of slaves owned by Quakers, had resolved that men of that faith should neither buy nor sell slaves. Individual Quakers, such as Anthony Benezet and John Woolman, had gone much farther in their publicized attacks. The other more radical Protestant sects, in seeking to dissociate themselves from a wicked world, had counted human slavery as an especially defiling sin from which they should turn away utterly. At the other extreme, the growth of more humanistically oriented religious attitudes among those convinced of the inherent goodness rather than the inherent sinfulness of man, and more concerned than Calvinists or Catholics with his earthly happiness, was also conducive to a humane concern about slavery.

Thus, the pre-Revolutionary attacks on the institution, in North America as in the Caribbean and in Latin America, were religious rather than political. Insofar as they were concerned with the Negro at all, they were concerned primarily with his status as a child of God or as an object of Christian charity rather than with his proper status under the law. The blacks' opportunity to receive religious instruction and to save their souls by conversion was much more important in the thought of the religious opponents of slavery than their right to legal or economic freedom. Increasingly in the late colonial and Revolutionary period a concern arose among a few religious leaders for the status of the blacks themselves, but in general the primary concern of the sects was the white man's freedom from sin rather than the black man's freedom from slavery. Even the Quakers were worried more about their own defilement by slavery than about the black man's imprisonment by it. It was sin above all things that was to be avoided, and it was the master, not the slave, who was threatened by sin.

But in the Revolutionary era the political and legal assertions of the equality of all men and their universal and equal right to freedom defined new issues. The inconsistency of this faith with the continued existence of slavery was repeatedly exposed and denounced, by Virginians as well as by New Englanders and by men of all varieties of religious belief. The concern was extended from the white man's soul to the black man's rights, and for the first time the attacks were on the institution of slavery itself rather than on the sins and cruelties associated with it.

The shocking contradiction between the professions of the Declaration and the practices of slavery, though it troubled relatively few of the national leaders, was repeatedly assaulted by ministers and pamphleteers. The Quaker David Cooper put it most bluntly in his *Serious Address on Slavery:* "If these solemn *truths,* uttered at such an awful crisis, are *self-evident:* unless we can show that the African race are not *men*, words can hardly express the amazement which naturally arises on reflecting, that the very people who make these pompous declarations are slave-holders, and, by their legislative conduct, tell us, that these blessings were only meant to be the rights of *white-men* not of all *men*. . . ." (As quoted in Winthrop Jordan, *White over Black*, p. 290.)

This dilemma drove those who could not bring themselves simply to ignore it into one of three positions. They could believe that all men were indeed created equal and with an unalienable right to liberty and that slavery must therefore be abolished. Or they could agree that slavery was morally and logically unjustifiable, but hold that it was the only present means of organizing the labor of ignorant blacks and of providing for their care, protection, training, and control, and that therefore, though an evil ultimately to be abolished, it was for the present a necessary evil. Or they could hold that Negroes were not men.

This last view was widely if usually tacitly held: that blacks, though perhaps in a technical sense biological members of the human species, were really so different from whites as to occupy a quite separate biological and therefore legal status. Though few apologists for slavery would have publicly asserted the doctrine of separate species in the late eighteenth century, critics of the institution remorsely pointed out that just this belief was the only means of reconciling slavery with the Revolutionary creed. As a Newport minister asserted in 1776, the colonists' education "has filled us with strong prejudices, against them [Negroes] and led us to consider them, not as our brethren, or in any degree on a level with us; *but as quite another species of animals*, made only to serve us and our children. . . ." (Samuel Hopkins in *A Dialogue Concerning the Slavery of the Africans; Shewing It to Be the Duty and Interest of the American Colonies to Emancipate All Their African Slaves*. Norwich, Connecticut, 1776, p. 34, as quoted in Jordan, *White over Black*, p. 276. Italics added.)

In the short run, the liberal enthusiasm of the Revolution substantially improved the position of Negroes. Slavery was ended in Northern states, where it had only a slight role in the economy. Following Pennsylvania's lead in 1780, Connecticut, Rhode Island, New York, and New Jersey all had passed emancipation acts in the next quarter-century, providing in most cases for gradual liberation over a period of time. Slavery was held unlawful by the courts in Massachusetts as being in contravention of its new Bill of Rights. It simply atrophied in New Hampshire. Emancipation was seriously, if unsuccessfully, advocated in Maryland, Delaware, and Virginia. The Northwest Ordinance in 1787 outlawed slavery in the national territories west of the mountains and north of the Ohio. The importation of slaves had been forbidden by the Continental Congress as a wartime economic measure, and most of the states subsequently continued this prohibition. Only Georgia never interrupted importation. The Constitution, drafted in 1787, tacitly recognized slavery but authorized Congress to bar the import of slaves after 1808. In the South, voluntary emancipation was made simpler. The legal status of the Negro in the 1790s was better than it would be again for three-quarters of a century.

But any optimism about the future of blacks in America arising from the liberal surge of the Revolutionary era was subject to serious qualification. At least three ominous portents emerged from the period. One was that liberalism prevailed against slavery or even threatened it only in states where the institution had lost its value to whites. In South Carolina and Georgia, where fresher soil, the revival of rice culture, and the long-staple cotton industry all made slave labor advantageous to its owners, there was an adamant resistance not only to the abolition of slavery but even to any discussion of its modification. If new economic developments should create new opportunities to exploit slave labor profitably elsewhere, a new zeal for slavery could be expected to follow.

In the second place, the debates over the drafting and ratification of the federal Constitution had made it clear that a national recognition and protection of slavery was the inescapable price that would have to be paid for Southern participation in the national union. As 1861 was to prove, this insistence was not a Southern bluff but a reality. There would be a United States of America in which black slavery was recognized, legitimized, and protected, or there would be no United States, or only a regional union of the Northern states. Hence the Constitution, though it managed to avoid any explicit use of the word, made it clear that the national government would be powerless to interfere with slavery within the states, that for twenty years it would be powerless to interfere even with the foreign trade in slaves, and that property in human beings would receive the same protection under the law as any other sort of property.

American nationhood was defined *ideologically* in the Declaration of Independence. We asserted that we became a nation *because* all men were created equal and were therefore entitled to certain unalienable rights, among them liberty, and the whole purpose of our nationhood was to assert that equality and secure those rights. As Lincoln was to say, we were a nation conceived in liberty and dedicated to the proposition that all men are created equal. But American nationhood was *legally* defined in a Constitution that recognized, clothed with lawful sanction, and protected inequality and the total and ultimate denial of liberty.

In every nation there is a tension between its ideology and its institutions, between the ideals and the realities of its life. Notions of British liberty and justice were in harsh contrast with the realities of British life in the eighteenth and nineteenth centuries; and liberty, equality, and fraternity were most imperfectly realized in French society in the decades following that nation's great Revolution. But because it was more rigid, more explicit, and more fundamental, the conflict between ideal and fact in American life was far more deeply irreconcilable. The United States was not an organic growth. Its nationhood was not based on a common descent or a long evolution. Two explicit acts created the nation: a Declaration of Independence that severed the North American commonwealths from Britain and a Constitution that united them into a nation. Hence, neither its ideals nor its institutions had the amorphous and undefined character that they might have had in a more traditional society. Here each was set forth in a clear and sharp-edged light. And they were not mere qualities or attributes of American society; they *created* that society. Equal liberty and human slavery were both essential and integral parts of the very definition of American nationhood as it was established in 1789.

But the most ominous portent was the path taken out of this dilemma—the dehumanization of the Negro. The more sensitive the white conscience to the evils of slavery, the more it was driven to find its justification in the denial of human rights to the blacks as a race. From the fanatical racist who insisted that Negroes were another species altogether, more akin to ape than to man, to the benign and paternal planter who smiled over the childlike irresponsibility of his "people" and who made wry jokes about their stupidity and need for direction, whites responded to the Revolution by quietly omitting blacks from the community of equal men who made up the nation.

CHAPTER THREE

In Which the Steam Engine, Which Enriched Whites, Revived the Slavery of Blacks

FOR CENTURIES cotton had provided fiber for the fine cloths of the Muslim world, and the hot American summers invited its culture. But not until the nineteenth century did it become an important American crop. By 1835, however, it had come to dominate the Southern economy and to be the basic staple of American foreign trade. Its export earned the foreign exchange on which the explosively rapid growth of the American economy in the nineteenth century was based. The shipload after shipload of cotton pouring into the docks of Liverpool financed the factories and railroads of the United States and the vast settlement of the West. In the economic life of nineteenth-century America, Cotton was indeed King.

This economic revolution is coupled in the popular mind with Eli Whitney's invention of the toothed cotton gin, which radically lowered the cost of removing the seed from the bolls of the short-staple varieties of cotton that were suited to upland farms. But in fact this simple device was a minor, if essential, factor in the cotton revolution. Roller gins adequate to remove the more easily separated seed from long-staple "sea island" cotton had long been known, and the development of a toothed variety was an obvious step that would be taken whenever it was needed.

The inventions that really crowned King Cotton were the power spinning frames and looms of Britain and New England and the steamboat and steam locomotive. These created an insatiable demand for cotton, opened a vast inland realm to commercial agriculture, and made possible the transatlantic movement of massive quantities of freight. Here was the perfect crop for slavery: cultivated by gangs, requiring little specialized skill, hardy, immune to then known diseases and pests, suitable to the soils and climate of most of the South, and enjoying a remunerative and apparently limitless market. Here was a staple that could be grown on millions of acres unsuited for tobacco, rice, or sugar. And as the steamboat made its way up the rivers and bayous and branching streams of the Mississippi Valley and as the iron tracks of the railroad moved into the Piedmont hills, a whole domain formerly impenetrable or useful only to the subsistence farmer was opened to the planter.

Settlements quickly filled the uplands of the Carolinas and Georgia and boiled out over Alabama, Mississippi, and western Tennessee. By the 1820s the Mississippi had been crossed and the settlement of Arkansas, Missouri, and northern Louisiana begun. A decade later settlers were sweeping into Texas. This was a new sort of frontier—not a trickle of individual pioneers clearing tiny fields, building one-room cabins, living on wild game and hastily grown corn, but a flood of entrepreneurs marching their columns of slaves through the wilderness to clear broad domains. The plantation house, crude at the beginning but from the first ample in size and power, was built over the still-warm ashes of Creek and Choctaw fires.

As the cotton boom roared toward its climax, the hungry demand for a massive, cheap, semiskilled labor force that could be held to its task amid all the temptations of the burgeoning frontier became as intense as during the eighteenth-century tobacco boom—and on a far larger scale. In the relatively liberal interval of the Revolutionary period, the Constitution had authorized the banning of slave importations after 1808, and this authority was promptly exercised. Although a considerable clandestine slave trade persisted throughout the following decades, it was never nearly adequate to supply the demand generated by the opening of the new cotton lands. The resulting major rise in the price of slaves revived the profitability of the institution even for those planters in the upper South who were unable to grow cotton or to employ their labor force efficiently on their own lands but who could export their surplus slaves to the new cotton belt.

We have seen that slavery had been introduced into American society in the colonial period without real thought to what was happening. Black unfree servants worked alongside white, the forms of indentured servitude gradually metamorphosed into those of chattel slavery, and a new and unplanned institution came into being. Slavery had existed for two generations before it became a matter of sufficient public concern to require the enactment of a slave code. Few men in the colonial period gave thought to the relation of slavery to the American destiny. The first serious questioning of the institution had come during the Revolutionary period. Most articulate men of that generation recognized the incompatibility between slavery and the conceptions of equality and liberty on which the nation's image of itself was based. But few thought the immediate abolition of slavery practical or had the courage to advocate it. Most saw the principal evil of slavery in the presence in America of a large, unassimilable mass of laborers who were believed to be ignorant, incapable of self-discipline and self-support, savage, and dangerous. Slavery was merely the unpleasant, if the most practical, means of organizing, training, and controlling the blacks and putting them to effective use. Though an admitted evil, slavery was thought to be a necessary one, of which the Americans could afford to be rid only when the black community was transformed in character or transported back to Africa. Yet however vaguely and distantly, the Revolutionary and immediately post-Revolutionary generations did look forward to a time, beyond slavery, when all 'Americans would indeed be equal and free—and preferably white—and American democracy could bring to full realization its true character unembarrassed by slavery or by the presence of the ominous and silently accusing black community.

All this changed with the coming of cotton. Slavery became again the indispensable basis of the Southern economy and of the plantation society which that economy engendered. It became in Southern eyes no longer an evil made necessary by the unfortunate presence of blacks but a positive good which made possible the organization of a stable society and a prosperous economy, assuring the status and dignity of all white men and the wealth of the dominant plantation owners. The long uncertainty of attitude was finally resolved in the 1830s. The Southern states in that decade revised their constitutions and systematized their slave codes with a view to the permanent and effective establishment of the slave system. The plantation as an organism for the use of blacks in agriculture was perfected. Extra-legal methods for the systematic control of blacks and for their preparation for the role of slaves were matured. Ideas relating to the education and training of blacks were altered from an ideal of preparing them for freedom to the ideal of conditioning them to view permanent and hereditary slavery, without hope of betterment ever, as an acceptable destiny for themselves and their children. Systematic defenses of slavery against subversive acts and subversive ideas, from within or from without the region, were devised. And a coherent rationalization of all this was elaborated, so that Southerners would be provided with the appropriate devices to square slavery with the political ideals of their country and the teachings of their religion and to answer the accusations of alien critics and of their own consciences. In the generation from 1835 to 1860 slavery reached its full maturity as an institution.

Slavery was legally defined as the absolute ownership of the person of the slave and of the offspring of a slave mother. The owner was required by law or by custom to provide food, clothing, shelter and medical care to his slaves, including children, the elderly, and the invalid. In return he was entitled to command their labor, to control their behavior, and to buy and sell them as property. Slavery was confined by custom if not by law to blacks, and a certain presumption existed that any black was a slave unless he could prove otherwise.

The master's absolute ownership was qualified by law in various ways. In many states very young children could not be separated by sale from their mothers. Although a master could whip a slave without limit and administer other severe and painful punishment, and although he was guiltless if the slave died in the course of punishment not intended to cause his death, the law forbade him to kill or maim a slave deliberately. The legal enforcement even of this limited provision was made ineffective by the fact that blacks, who were likely to be the only witnesses of such crimes, could not testify against whites. Custom and community sentiment, however, provided a considerable protection of most slaves against extremes of physical abuse.

The principal limitations of the absolute rights of the master were aimed at curbing not his brutality but his indulgence of his slaves. In all or most Southern states, for example, a master might not teach or permit others to teach his slaves to read or write. He could not lawfully permit them to meet for religious or other purposes except in the presence of a white man or to bear arms except when specifically authorized to hunt. Most important of all, his right to free his slaves was progressively narrowed so that by the 1850s manumission without a special act of the legislature had become almost impossible. Slaves were not permitted to be off their owners' premises without a pass, and patrols were required by law to enforce curfews on blacks. The enforcement of many of these provisions was casual in quiet times but was likely to be severe whenever there were rumors of slave uprisings. And the latent power was always there.

Slaves themselves had almost no civil existence under the law. They could not sue or be sued, or testify in a case involving whites, or own property, or contract a legal marriage, or serve on a jury, or vote. They had no legal protection against whipping, branding, or similar physical punishment by their masters and no effective protection against even more brutal treatment; yet severe penalties, even death, awaited a slave who raised his hand against a white, however desperate the provocation.

But the organization and control of a servile labor force at this time of American history could not be achieved by law alone. Slavery reached its final and rigid form in the Jacksonian era of the common man and in the years when the vast treasure house of the West was opened wide to exploitation. A fervor of optimism possessed the American people. Save for the sharp depression following the Panic of 1837, these were flush years, when the dream of wealth lay open to every man's ambitions. They were the years the steamboat and the railroad made an entire people mobile, when Texas and California and Oregon and the vastness of the Western mountain empire fell to American arms and diplomacy, and the wagon trains moved endlessly, bringing men and women to settle them.

They were decades, too, of a generous upwelling of democratic and humanitarian sentiment—the era, in Alice

Tyler's phrase, of freedom's ferment. The whole of America was permeated by the boisterous conviction that one man was as good as another in a churning, fluid society that opened overflowing opportunity to all. The years in which slavery was most firmly fixed in American life were the years of Emerson and Thoreau.

To preserve in the midst of this ferment an institution so alien to the rest of American life required an enormous, diligent, and unwearying effort. Slaves could not be controlled and made to work productively by naked force alone. They had to be compelled to an acceptance, however sullen and reluctant, of a role for themselves and their children and their children's children forever in which the whole burgeoning promise America offered everyone else was totally denied. And Southerners had to justify this institution to the rest of America and to their own consciences. The means used were effective but costly beyond measure to the white society that used them.

It was necessary above all to keep hope from the blacks. This was not easy to do in a society built on hope, bursting with dreams of the wealth and power and happiness that would come from the exploitation of the vast continent it was reaching out to occupy. It required as nearly as possible the insulation of the Negro from all the currents of thought coursing around him. The ideal of the controllers of the slave society was to have blacks isolated on plantations, where they would never see a Negro who was not a slave or a white who was not a master, so that the roles of the two races would seem to be their respective inexorable destinies. The control of the movements of slaves was intended not only to prevent their escape or their meeting to conspire but to limit as much as possible their contacts and sources of information.

There were, of course, slaves in cities, usually employed as domestic servants, and slaves who were hired out by their owners to work alongside free black and even white men as artisans or factory hands. But conservative sentiment deplored this liberality, and in many localities ordinances forbade allowing slaves to live or work under conditions having the aspects of freedom. A prudent slaveowner kept his servants as remote from contact with the outside world as possible.

The cutting off of communication was enforced in other ways as well. Not only was no provision made for Negro education, but positive legislation in most states made it a crime to teach a slave to read and write. The books and newspapers of the day, vibrant with the expansive freedom of the nineteenth century, were not for him. Religious ideas might be particularly dangerous, and the religious exercises of slaves were closely supervised. Preaching to slaves was supposed to be carried on only with the approval of the master and in the presence of a white man, who could be sure that the message dealt only with happiness in the next world and the necessity of humility and obedience in this life as a means to salvation in the next. Any gathering of blacks without the presence of a white man was forbidden for whatever purpose. Many of these strictures were intended to control plotting and conspiracy among the blacks; but they had the effect of limiting communication of every kind, so that slaves had only a meager chance to know the meaning of freedom or the nature of the world outside their neighborhood, or to envision a different life for themselves, or to make a concrete and realistic plan to achieve it.

Ambition was stifled systematically. A slave could not hope for freedom or wealth or even modest means. He could get nothing for the hardest work beyond his master's praise and perhaps to be named a driver and boss a gang of his fellow slaves. Weariness was the only end of extra labor. Indeed, the plantation system, where slaves worked in a gang all at the same pace or at tasks assigned by a standard pattern capable of relatively easy completion, did little to require unusual effort, much less to reward it.

Nor was the slave driven by the need for security. Lazy or industrious, thrifty or improvident, his minimal needs for food, clothing, and shelter would be taken care of; and nothing he could do would gain him more. He need feel no responsibility for wife or children. His utmost labors could not better their lot; his courage could not protect them; his negligence would not leave them homeless or unclothed or hungry. Any determination to better himself, to progress toward freedom, to seize on learning, to bear himself with dignity was likely to be thought the mark of a dangerous "uppity nigger" and to bring him not praise or respect but the whip. Every basic belief of that ambitious, hopeful, buoyant, driving century was obliterated or turned on its head when applied to the slave.

The family, which was the principal stable social structure in a society so fluid and atomistic as that of nineteenth-century America, was attenuated in slavery. Though "weddings" of slaves were recognized by most masters and sometimes solemnized by the church, marriage as a civil contract was impossible to slaves, and family relationships among slaves were often unstable and temporary. Fathers and mothers had no legal responsibility for their children, who were provided for by the master, and no final authority over them, as they were subject to the master's control and discipline. A slave was powerless to protect his wife or children against whipping or other punishment by their owner, or against sexual abuse by him, or even against their sale to a distant owner. The intensely moralistic society of the period imposed no requirement of chastity on slaves. Though owners might try to insist on such stability in sexual pairings among their slaves as would avoid jealousy and fighting, there was no insistence that the sexual appetites of slaves be curbed, any more than those of any animal the master owned. In the white mythology blacks were in any case animal-like in their sensuality, and restraint could not be expected; marriage among slaves was a meaningless institution; if their lust was sated among their own kind it was less likely to be dangerously directed toward white women; and the children born of slaves, whether begot in stable unions or not, were not an embarrassment or a shame but a valuable asset to their owner.

But this effort at devaluation of the family among slaves was not primarily a concession to what was thought to be black sensuality and irresponsibility. It was a deliberate and necessary object of white policy. If black fathers and not their owners had had authority over slave children, if the relationship between a slave husband and wife had been respected by the state, the power of the owner to dispose of the labor and persons of his slaves would have been seriously limited.

But there was an even more important way in which the disruption of the family life of slaves was central to the effectiveness of white policy. Innocent though they were of knowledge of modern psychology, the whites nevertheless hit upon the surest means of shaping slaves to their will. We have learned the extraordinary importance of parents in affording models on which children can shape their images of themselves. Whites took care to see that the image of his father before the eyes of any boy growing up a slave was not of a man but of a slave, unable to protect or control his family, not able to provide their support, not having the freedom or bearing the responsibility of a husband or a father or a man, helpless to assert his own dignity or to protect that of his wife or children before the rule of a master. Generation after generation of slave children were reared, deliberately reared, in this self-destroying image of impotence, hopelessness, irresponsibility, and personal degradation. It was a device far more subtle and effective than the lash in the effort to create a hopeless, submissive, and manageable labor force.

It is a profound tribute to the fortitude and integrity of the slave men and women that in the face of this consistent assault, over generations, they were so often able to maintain a continuity of family life that preserved the core of values on which a free black society could ultimately be erected.

The church as well, that other great organizing force in nineteenth-century American society, was so drastically altered as to lose most of its social meaning for blacks. Owners welcomed the religious instruction of slaves and their expression of religious feeling, so long as it was directed toward the humble fulfillment of obligations in this life and the anticipation of rewards in the next. For whites most Protestant congregations were a means of mobilizing and directing emotions, providing a union and structure for social efforts and a medium for self-definition. But any such function of the church as an autonomous social body was completely denied to blacks. There was no chance for the slave and almost none for the free black to unite with his fellows in a self-governing body that could provide a shape and a voice for his feelings, an instrument for his public action, and an organism within which he could grow and find expression.

And, of course, slaves had no part in the political and social processes that did so much to shape the character of white society in the antebellum decades. Democratic government, especially at the local level, the rotation of local office-holding, service on juries, membership in the militia and participation in its training exercises were all powerful instruments in educating whites and shaping white society. From all of these experiences all slaves and indeed almost all black freemen were totally excluded.

As a result of this comprehensive and all-embracing process of character-shaping, white society was able to fetter the slave with bonds far more confining and far more permanent than any of iron and leather. The institutions of white society which Tocqueville described were all designed to produce men alert, informed, hopeful, ambitious, mobile, driving in energy, self-seeking but schooled in cooperation and association, used to self-government, reared in stable family units, self-expressive, finding in religion not a creed imposed by authority but a means by which men could join to assert their own views of human character and destiny. Whites sought, and with remarkable success, to maintain the enslavement of blacks by a pattern of training calculated to produce precisely the opposite traits in those they claimed to own. To produce a class willing to acquiesce, however sullenly and resentfully, in a relationship that denied them and their posterity forever both freedom for their persons and reward for their labors and that placed their very beings at the command of others required the opposite in every way of the pattern of training of American whites of that century. The institution demanded beings dull, ignorant, fixed in place and status, without hope or ambition, seeking neither self-expression nor self-government, organized in no groupings of family or church that might unite the energies of the slaves or stand between the individual slave and his master. To shape character in that pattern in Jacksonian America was a remarkable, an almost incredible, feat, possible only by the exercise of great skill and psychological insight, of iron will, and of long and persistent application. But the masters of slave society achieved something surprisingly close to success.

To make the system work, it was necessary to shape the whites as well as the blacks. Liberty and equality were basic and ardently held principles of the Jacksonian years. "The era of the common man" it has been called. Hundreds of thousands of whites had to be helped to square these principles of liberty and equality with their buying, selling, and owning other men. So far as slave-holders were concerned, the task of persuasion was made much easier by the benefits they derived from being able to command the use of unpaid labor. But the virtues of slavery were less obvious to nonslaveholding Southern whites. They grew cotton with their own labors and sold it in competition with that grown by slaves; they were pushed into the unfertile uplands and the distant hill country by planters whose wealth enabled them to monopolize the best cotton lands; they compared their poor clothing, inadequate housing, and meager funds with the arrogant wealth wrung from slave labor; they lived under state and local governments dominated by men of wealth whose leisure and education, again based on slave labor, enabled them to hold commanding positions over their neighbors. Even less were the advantages of slavery obvious to Northerners, whose states had long since abolished the institution, who had little experience of Negroes, and whose representatives encountered in Washington a consolidated and powerful political interest, again based on slavery, and hostile at major points to Northern interests.

A varied complex of arguments was developed to rationalize slavery to these various groups. There were two possible lines of reasoning. One could accept the egalitarian and libertarian bases of the American tradition but deny that they extended to blacks. Though all but extremists were willing enough to grant the humanity of Negroes, almost all Americans, Southerners and Northerners alike, were convinced that they were congenitally of a far lower order of intelligence, foresight, and character than whites and hence were unfit to enjoy the privileges or accept the responsibilities of free men. Leaders as liberal as Thomas Jefferson and Abraham Lincoln shared this view. In his debates with Douglas in 1858 and elsewhere, Lincoln affirmed that he was "not in favor of the social and political equality of the white and black races," opposed Negro suffrage and held that the "physical differences" of the races would "forever forbid" their "living together on terms of social and political equality." In these views he followed Jefferson himself, who thought Negroes congenitally far inferior to whites in reason, forethought, and aesthetic creativity.

The visible evidence, of course, seemed to support these views. The slave population, stripped of their own culture and denied access to any but the most rudimentary elements of their masters', were, with occasional exceptions, in fact simple and ignorant. And to whites of Jefferson's class whose educational opportunities, formal and informal, had been immeasurably superior, they appeared stupid as well. The careful suppression of ambition and the denial of rewards to foresight and thrift had had their intended effect. Most Americans simply took it for granted that blacks were so different from whites as to be outside the meaning of the Declaration and the Constitution. They were not parts of the political community to which the liberal and egalitarian canons of the American tradition applied. The relatively primitive character of African society, as it was reported in the colorful accounts of nineteenth-century missionaries, confirmed these impressions of black incapacity.

Negroes were thought not only unintelligent and improvident but also wild and dangerous. The African tribesman was envisioned as a fierce and cannibalistic savage. The atrocities accompanying the black revolution in Haiti, exaggerated in report, ominously frightened American whites; and their fears were heightened by the occasional bloody uprisings of American slaves. The most famous of these, that led by Nat Turner in southeastern Virginia in 1831, came just at the time when Southern constitutions and slave codes were hardening into their final antebellum shape. Adding to the Southern fears was the persistent belief in a fierce and uncontrollable black sexuality.

For all of these reasons, slavery, however repugnant to American ideals of liberty and equality, was justified as a necessary arrangement for blacks, to give useful organization to their labor, to provide for their own care and sustenance, and to control them for the protection of the white community.

But there were those who went further, denied the values of egalitarianism, and justified slavery as a desirable institution in itself, quite apart from any special incapacity on the part of Negroes. These men, of whom George Fitzhugh, author of *Cannibals All*, was the most thoughtful, held the view that no high civilization was possible except at the cost of enforced labor by unrewarded masses. Only such an arrangement could provide the surplus that would give an elite the leisure to pursue learning and the arts and to attain the full dignity of man's estate. In the highest cultures of the past, in Egypt, Israel, Greece, and Rome, such labor had been provided by slaves and in medieval and early modern times by serfs. In the Northern states and in Great

Britain it was provided in the cruelest way of all, by factory hands who labored far harder than slaves, for no better level of subsistence, and without protection against old age, sickness, or unemployment.

Slavery, such thinkers held, was the most benign of all means of organizing the labor of the masses, providing the employer with a stable and dependable labor force and the employee with assurance of continuous support, while freeing the class of masters to pursue the higher purposes of the state, of culture and learning, and of religion. Though they believed that slavery was a valid form of organization for any society and even that enslavement would have bettered the lives of Irish peasants or factory laborers of the Northern states and Great Britain, the proslavery advocates thought it uniquely fitted to the Southern situation. Four million Negroes provided a body of men born, in their view, to be slaves. Their presence made it possible for all white men, and not merely a select few, to belong to the class of masters, whether in fact they owned slaves or not. With blacks supplying the mudsills of the state, the silent unrewarded mass of laborers which they believed must support any society, all whites could indeed be free and equal.

These elaborately rational bodies of argument, as developed in the works of such writers as Thomas Dew and George Fitzhugh, were probably less effective in soothing Southern consciences than were the reassurances of the Southern churches. By the early 1840s most major Protestant denominations had divided on sectional lines largely over the issue of slavery, and condemnation of the institution was almost entirely absent from Southern pulpits. On the contrary, the Southern churches, searching the Old Testament for references to ancient slavery, claimed a divine sanction for the practice. Going further, by depicting slavery as a means of uplifting the ignorant, savage, and heathen black, they were able to persuade the readily convinced slaveholder that he was doing the Lord's work. Civilizing the black, removing him from the brutality, danger, and suffering of the jungle to the safety and serenity of the plantation, suffering patiently and indulgently his shortcomings, providing for him in infancy, illness, and old age, opening to him the means of saving his immortal soul—the slaveholder could see himself, if he were so inclined, as a benign and long-suffering instrument of divine mercy.

Though slavery attained its classic form in the large plantation, the majority of slaveholders were in fact townspeople and yeomen farmers, who might own one or two house servants or a half dozen or fewer farm helpers. By 1860, 25 percent of the white families in the South owned one or more slaves. This was the most powerful argument binding the whites outside the planter class to its support. Nonslaveholding whites, the poor farmers of the back country, the landless laborers, the city artisans and workmen were likely to resent and fear Negroes as economic competitors and to despise and wish to degrade them as a way to reinforce their own relative social elevation. They resented them further as an unfair means by which planters were able to achieve an economic and social dominance over lesser whites. But in a society with millions of blacks, the poor whites were determined to keep them enslaved as a means of keeping them down and safely below the lowest white man.

The presence of blacks as a dangerous threat to the safety of all white men, women, and children was argued as a further reason for white solidarity. A sense of fraternity was engendered among whites of all classes as they were pressed to obey a common code in dealing with the blacks. As this code was based on the subservience of all blacks, slave or free, whatever their station or character, to whites, however poor or ignorant, it appealed especially to the vanity of just those whites whose economic interests were most at variance with those of the planters. The more his economic position resembled that of the free black or even the slave, the more eagerly the poor white seized on the pathetic identification with the master class afforded by his skin color and joined in the support of slavery.

The early 1830s marked a watershed in opinions of slavery, North as well as South. The renewed profitability of the institution resulting from the opening of the rich cotton lands of Alabama and Mississippi had crystallized the shifting and ambivalent views of the South and had determined a Southern policy to demand complete protection of slave property and interests by the national government in the national territories as well as the Southern states. From a defensive attitude toward slavery as a temporarily necessary evil the South shifted to an aggressive praise of the institution as a socially desirable arrangement which they were absolutely determined to expand and make permanent.

The latter 1830s and the 1840s and 1850s saw a reciprocal hardening of Northern views. Prior to the 1830s, though there was a general distaste for slavery in the North and though it had been abolished in those states, the sons and grandsons of the generations that had actually carried on the slave trade from Newport and Boston had come to no deep moral conviction about its eradication in the South. With the founding of the American Anti-Slavery Society in 1833, and the first publication of William Lloyd Garrison's *The Liberator* in 1831, there came into being the organs of a persistent and broadening campaign aimed at the confinement and ultimate abolition of slavery. Shrilly, persistently, unequivocally, endlessly, the abolitionists hammered at the total sinfulness of slavery and demanded that its destruction transcend every other object of national policy, even the preservation of the Union itself.

Their propaganda greatly heightened the tensions over the slavery issue and no doubt contributed to the steeling of Northern sentiment when the Civil War came. But it never commanded a majority support in the North, even at the beginning of the war itself, and not until near the war's end did national sentiment solidify behind the abolition of slavery. On the contrary, the abolitionists were regarded throughout most Northern circles as disagreeable and intemperate radicals and were heckled, harassed, assaulted, and even killed by Northern mobs. In spite of their dwindling minority in the population and in Congress, the Southerners, with Northern support or acquiescence, were able to assure themselves that national policy would respect and protect the interests of slaveholders.

The extraordinary success of Southern publicists in averting determined Northern action against slavery was due to a number of causes. Perhaps foremost was the fact that almost all Northerners accepted as did Southerners the inherent inferiority of Negroes. Even many abolitionists appeared to be moved more by hostility to slaveholders and to the institution of slavery as a sin and an offense to American political ideals than by any affection or sympathy for the enslaved blacks. Proposals for abolition were frequently coupled with proposals for the banishment of the freedmen to Africa in order to rid America of their presence. Indeed one of the underlying reasons for the hostility to slavery on the part of many of its opponents was that it had been responsible for bringing into the country the blacks on whom they looked with fear and contempt. Only a handful of voices were raised in the North to assert the equal humanity of blacks and to seek their equal participation in American life. Among the great majority of Northerners this aversion to blacks mitigated any opposition they might have had to slavery itself and induced them to tolerate Southern actions in dealing with a problem they would not have been willing to face themselves.

Moreover, profound respect for the absolute rights of the owners of property was one of the fundamental political convictions of nineteenth-century America. Property, equally with life and liberty, was guaranteed by the Bill of Rights itself, and these three rights, as an inextricably linked trilogy, were endlessly repeated in the political discourse of the time. Once the concept of slaves as property was accepted, a whole train of consequent beliefs arose in the minds of all right-thinking Northerners to protect the rights of ownership. Abolition was viewed with horror as an expropriation of the slaveholders' property; the apprehension and return of escaping slaves was thought a moral as well as a legal duty; and Northern businessmen, even though unsympathetic to slavery, were troubled by any denial of the right of a man of means to take his property with him into any of the newly opening national territories, even if that property consisted of slaves.

Finally, it was clear, as 1861 proved, that no effective action could be taken against slavery without civil war or the destruction of the Union. An occasional Garrison might denounce the Constitution as a covenant with Hell, but to almost all Northerners, as to Abraham Lincoln, the problem of slavery was entirely secondary to the preservation of the Union. Recognizing their inability to end or even limit slavery at a cost they were willing to pay, Northerners resented those who sought to force them to face the moral aspects of their acquiescense and were impelled to find reasons to justify their inaction. These they tended to find in a recognition of the legal rights of slaveholders and a sympathetic view of Southern arguments for the necessity of slavery as a means of controlling blacks.

This combination of power, rationalization, arguments, and appeals was extraordinarily successful for a time. Blacks themselves were for the most part held quiescent by force, hopelessness, ignorance, and deliberate destruction of any sources of organization and leadership. Small farmers were identified with the slaveholding class by the ownership of one or two workers or a family. Except for the mountain areas, even poorer whites were drawn to the ardent defense of slavery by seeing it as a means of enforcing their shabby superiority over the blacks. Southern dissent was forcibly stilled, and Northern abolitionism was rendered politi cally impotent. The Southern slaveholders were not only able to preserve the institution long past its abolition throughout almost all the civilized world but to reinforce its status by a more stringent fugitive slave law, by Supreme Court decisions affirming the rights of slaveholders, and by a series of acts and decisions progressively removing the restrictions on slavery in the territories that had been first imposed in the Northwest Ordinance of 1787, leaving slavery free to expand to its utmost geographic limits. Meanwhile the Northern and European demand for cotton seemed insatiable as cotton mills sprang daily into being. Except for occasional setbacks in years of panic, such as 1837 or 1857, the slave system thrived in ever more arrogant power.

But the maintenance of this power to use blacks as slaves had cost the South dearly. The capital and the entrepreneurial energy of the region was frozen in cotton planting. However enriching to the successful planter, it was an impoverishing drain on the region. Though commercial conventions met from time to time throughout the antebellum period in the South to agitate for the development of Southern industry, they were not really interested in truly independent industrial growth such as that which in Great Britain and the northeastern states was displacing agriculture as the dominant element in the economy. What they wanted was a subservient industry that would serve the ends of the plantation system by supplying more cheaply the supplies and equipment it required. The railroad network of the cotton states, like those of the colonial economies of Africa and Latin America, was designed not for internal development but primarily for the speedy movement to ports of the one export staple. The banking system as well, rudimentary in its development, was almost entirely addressed to the special needs of large-scale agriculture and had but scant association with industrial or commercial development. The new industrial growth in the Northeast and the cities of the Midwest commanded the bursting energies of the ablest and most dynamic elements of the economy; advocates of true industrialization in the South were an almost powerless minority, strangers to rather than leaders of the dominant economic forces. Their plans were crippled by dearth of capital and stifled under the devotion of the region to the plantation economy. Abortive efforts were made to use slaves in factories or on railroads in the South, but most of the attempts were soon abandoned except for their employment in railroad construction and in iron manufacture at Richmond. Slaves proved adaptable enough to factory work, but slavery was not. The more successful a Negro workman proved himself in a factory the more he shed the attributes of slavery. Moving back and forth in a money economy, having opportunities to practice ingenuity and initiative and foresight, employed in an occupation that did not surround his entire life womblike, as did the plantation society, he emerged from the inarticulate mass of slavery and became a man. Exposed to the general flow of ideas through town and factory and coming in contact with all manner of men and opinions rather than isolated in the self-contained ignorance of the plantation community, he was likely, moreover, to become a man with ideas and words to shape them. It was the unsuitability of slavery, not the unsuitability of Negroes, for manufacturing and commerce that turned Southerners away from the use of slaves in the new economic enterprises. Slaveholders and their slaves were fettered together in the prison of the cotton plantation.

But the imprisonment was not economic only. It was as necessary for whites to insulate themselves from the open world of thought as it was for them to isolate their slaves. Christianity became an intolerable doctrine unless translated into Southern Christianity, and in the 1840s Southern Baptist and Methodist congregations seceded from their national groups and formed Southern denominations whose ministers and teachings would not question the rightness of the Southern course and would call God and the Bible to the defense of human slavery. An earlier theological schism in the Presbyterian Church took on a similar regional pattern. Legislation and the free use of violence stopped the dissemination of antislavery writings in the South, and such Southern periodicals as *DeBow's Review* and *The Southern Literary Messenger* replaced national journals. The bonds of attachment to the nation and of intellectual communication with the outer world were snapped. Within the Union that had been conceived by Jefferson, created by Washington, given form by Madison and Marshall and sustained by Jackson, their heirs had become a tense, embittered, inward-looking minority, ready to deny the hopes, suppress the ideas, and destroy the work of the Founders if necessary to maintain their ways of using blacks.

Within the South itself a deadening denial of freedom of thought was enforced with increasing rigidity. As late as 1832 William Gaston, the Chief Justice of North

Carolina, could be loudly applauded when in a commencement address at the state university he vigorously attacked slavery as an evil burden; but more than twenty-five years later the mere expression of an intention to vote the Republican ticket was enough to cause a professor to be dismissed from the same university and driven beyond the very bounds of the state. To argue publicly for the abolition of slavery or even for its limitation in the South of the 1840s and 1850s was to invite not only verbal abuse, dismissal from any school or pulpit, and social ostracism, but physical violence as well.

The insistence on orthodoxy was not confined to ideas about slavery itself. The domains of science, religion, history, law, and political theory were rigidly policed, lest ideas be promulgated whose implications could ultimately threaten slavery. A sterile fundamentalism dominated the churches. History became an exercise in pious antiquarianism. Political theory, brilliantly elaborated by John Calhoun, became a series of fortifications to defend the peculiar arrangements of Southern society against both hostile attack and internal change. Where once the doors of Monticello stood open to all the free winds of the world's thought, the Southern mind turned inward to a narrow, sterile, obsessed determination not only to close out alien thought but also to deny any dynamism within itself that might thrust against its increasing rigidity.

The most serious and lasting damage to the white South, however, came not from these imposed limitations but from the transformation in individual whites wrought by their training in slavery. Just as the system worked implacably and effectively to leave the

black community structureless, leaderless, and emptied
of drives toward freedom and self-assertion, so it worked
equally implacably to distort white character toward
masterdom. So effectively were the convictions necessary to the support of slavery internalized that external
compulsion on Southern whites was rarely necessary.
Religious and kindly men came to see no evil in the
buying, selling, and owning of other men. Generous
men, who would share their last possession with a stran-
ger, were willing unhesitatingly to live on the compelled
and unrewarded labor of slaves. Men who thought themselves devoted to the doctrines of the Declaration and
of Christianity took for granted the inerasable otherness
and inherent and utter inferiority of a whole race and
complacently accepted the convictions of their own difference and superiority. They thought themselves per-
forming a duty when they rigidly insisted on black subservience in every relation of life. They came not only
to accept but to ennoble these practices, so that they saw
the Southern way of life as generous, democratic, dignified with responsibility, and sweetened by a tradition
of kindly justice. In time they would with selfless courage offer their lives, their fortunes, the whole panoply
of their lives to defend this system, dedicating to it their
finest qualities of loyalty and fortitude. And they were
to do so with willingness and pride, the most crippled
and deformed of all the victims of slavery.

CHAPTER FOUR

In Which War Changes the Means by Which Blacks Are Held to Labor

As the 1840s and 1850s passed, slavery seemed ever more firmly rooted in the law and the economy of the United States. The growing railroad network opened hundreds of thousands of new acres to cotton culture by providing a means of hauling bales to ports or factories. Millions upon millions of dollars were invested in new cotton mills in Old England and New. The constantly improving steamship brought the products of Manchester and New England looms to the entire world. Two decades of almost unbroken prosperity lifted the slave economy to the peak of its economic success.

With this success came an increasing political arrogance. Where once slaveholders were content to be left undisturbed in their home states to deal with an institution they themselves deplored, they now insisted ever more demandingly that property in slaves be protected throughout the Union and its territories. The policy embodied in the Missouri Compromise of 1820, which had been thought to settle the question of the expansion of slavery by limiting it to territories below the 36th parallel, had been demolished by the Compromise of 1850, the Kansas–Nebraska Act of 1854 and the Dred Scott decision of 1857, which opened all the territories to slavery and denied the Constitutional power of Congress to limit the right of any slaveholder to be protected in the ownership of his human property in any of the federal territories.

Meanwhile the annexation of Texas and the subsequent war with Mexico, both supported by proslavery political leaders and opposed by antislavery forces, had enormously increased the area in which slave labor might realistically be employed. Not content with this, the more zealous of the slavery party pressed for further expansion to the South, hungry for Cuba, Central America, and Mexico itself. Even the legal reopening of the never wholly suppressed African slave trade was seriously advocated.

Even more offensive to Northern sentiment was the Fugitive Slave Act, passed as a part of the Compromise of 1850, which required the officers of Northern states to put themselves at the service of slavery, capturing and returning to their owners escaped slaves who had reached free states. The act, moreover, gave no effective protection to free blacks who might be seized by slave-catchers on flimsy evidence and who might not be able to prove their freedom. Its operation brought evidence of the harshness of slavery home to residents of communities throughout the North who might otherwise never have seen the institution at first hand.

This arrogance extended even to the discussion of slavery. A gag rule in the Congress forbade even the consideration of petitions for the abolition of slavery. Southern postmasters were given the authority to refuse to distribute abolitionist literature entrusted to the mails. Wherever possible, Southerners endeavored to silence antislavery voices on the national scene as well as in the Southern states themselves. Increasingly, Southerners were insisting that their peculiar institution be given a special position, beyond the reach of law and beyond debate.

The very intensity of this insistence betrayed, however, a growing anxiety for the future of slavery. Though the majority of Northerners were little disposed to interfere in the institutions of another region and indeed resented abolitionists as shrill and intolerant troublemakers, the number of their fellows who found slavery offensive grew steadily. The abolitionist movement, never large in numbers but zealous, articulate, and determined, pressed its relentless attack from the mid-1830s onward. As the shadow of slavery fell over the Western territories to which men had looked as the expanding home of freedom, farmers all over the North began to feel oppressed and limited in their own opportunities. World opinion too turned steadily against the South as slaves were freed throughout the British, Spanish, and French empires. Like South Africans or Rhodesians of a later day, Southerners withdrew into a kraal of bitter and self-sufficient defense. And like the South Africans and Rhodesians, they chose ultimately to secede from a union in which their interests seemed threatened and their institutions were viewed with odium.

The Southern anxiety had been sharply increased by the dwindling of its power, influence, and relative wealth within the Union. However profitable slavery might be for the large slaveholder, it froze the economy of the region as a whole in a pattern of devastating impoverishment. In 1789, commonwealths like Virginia and South Carolina were among the richest in the Union. By 1860 the spread of factories, railroads, and cities across the face of the North had carried it generations beyond the relatively static economy of the cotton states. The German and Irish immigration that flowed into Northern ports and to Northern farms and cities shunned the domain of slavery. Freedom of thought was frozen in the same prison with economic enterprise, and Southern intellectual life, which had been so vital and creative in the days of Jefferson, Madison, and Marshall, dwindled to a fretful and barren defense of Southern racial patterns.

However hysterically it might offer denial, the South was aware of its waning strength and of its steadily more evident economic and intellectual inferiority; and it grew ever more fearful of the threat of Northern dominance.

The breaking point came with Lincoln's victory in the election of 1860. This brought to power the recently formed Republican party, which represented only Northern interests and was pledged to the confinement of slavery within its existing boundaries. Although Lincoln and his colleagues made it elaborately clear that they did not seek the abolition of slavery within the slave states and were even willing to give firm guarantees of its protection there, the more extreme Southern commonwealths felt that their interests were no longer secure and carried out at last their often repeated threat of secession. It soon became obvious that the dispute would not be peacefully resolved and that the Northern states would neither entice the seceding commonwealths to return by offering further concessions nor permit them to resign from the Union peacefully. When the inevitability of war was clear, the upper Southern slave states, save for Delaware, Maryland, Kentucky, and Missouri, joined the deep South in a new Confederacy. The United States was plunged into its bitterest and bloodiest war, the most traumatic event of its history.

All knew, then and now, that slavery was at the bottom of all the causes that led to secession and war. And yet the relation was ambiguous. The South denied that it fought primarily to preserve slavery. The North denied, with more sincerity, that it fought to abolish slavery. Lincoln, indeed, was constantly solicitous of the interests of slaveholders in the border states that remained within the Union, fearful lest they too be driven to secession. As clearly as English speech could state, he set forth the total subordination of antislavery motives to the one objective of preserving the Union:

"My paramount object in this struggle is to save the Union. . . . If I could save the Union without freeing any slave I would do it, and if I could save it by freeing all the slaves, I would do it; and if I could save it by freeing some and leaving others alone I would also do that. What I do about slavery, and the colored race, I do because I believe it helps to save the Union. . . ."

Beyond a mild distaste for the institution, most Northerners were indifferent to slavery except as it thrust itself upon them by intrusion in the territories or by operation of the Fugitive Slave Law within the free states or, finally, as it became the basis of secession. To the degree Northerners *were* hostile to slavery, it was most often because of their resentment of the slaveholder, not because of their sympathy with the slave. Northern arms, after years of bloody war, emerged totally triumphant, and the victors were free to redefine the role of blacks in American society. But they stood fumbling and indecisive before this opportunity. They had fought for four years, expended billions of dollars and given up hundreds of thousands of lives in a war all of whose causes were intertwined with the status of blacks in the United States, yet they had given little thought and had come to no decisions as to what that status ought to be.

Indeed, it was far from clear during the first two years of the war that slavery itself would be ended. Four slave states remained in the Union, and Lincoln was anxious to reassure slaveholders among their citizens that their support of the Union need not mean the confiscation of their property. Northern Democrats who were willing to fight for the preservation of the Union would have been reluctant to support a war for the abolition of slavery in view of their long contention that every state had a right to determine that question for itself. There was even hope that without total victory, the Southern states could be induced the more readily to return to a Union in which slavery would still be protected. Though the radical wing of the Republican party from the first saw the war as the destroyer of slavery, it was less their pressure than the force of military necessity that in fact brought freedom.

From the beginning of the war Union commanders operating along the coasts and borders of the Confederacy found their camps overrun by blacks who had fled their masters or had been left ownerless. Benjamin Butler, commanding in the Norfolk area, first hit on the idea of defining them as contraband of war and putting them to work for the Union army. Legal sanction was given this course by the Confiscation Act of August 6, 1861, which provided that slaves would be confiscated and freed if they had been used by their masters in the service of the Confederacy, a use that could be presumed in the case of most slaves who had escaped to Union lines.

But Lincoln had approved the act only with reluctance and firmly checked measures that went beyond its letter. General John Frémont, who had been the Republican candidate for President in 1856, was overruled when, in August 1861, he proclaimed martial law in Missouri and declared all slaves freed whose owners had actively aided the Confederacy. So was Secretary of War Cameron when, in his annual report of November 1861, he recommended the arming of Negroes and their use in the Union forces.

Lincoln recognized, however, that slavery had become an impossible anachronism, and he sought a means to put it on the road to extinction without alienating the border slaveholders or frightening those conservative Northerners who feared a black horde freed from the bonds of slavery. Lincoln's plan was to provide federal funds to reimburse any slave state for the expense of a program of compensated emancipation that would end slavery by 1900. Emancipation would be followed by a massive program of emigration under which freedmen would be conveyed to Africa or to tropical America and fostered by American support until they could create self-sustaining communities. The first step in this plan, the bill authorizing the funding of compensated emancipation, was proposed and enacted in the spring of 1862, and in April of that year Congress decreed such emancipation in the District of Columbia, where it could act directly.

But Lincoln's program met no further successes. The border states rejected even compensated emancipation, and the impracticality of black emigration was made evident by diplomatic rebuffs and by the total failure of a Central American experiment. The issue of slavery would have to be dealt with without the cooperation of the slaveholders or the disappearance of the freed blacks.

Congress continued to press more rapidly than Lincoln. In June and July 1862 it provided for the uncompensated emancipation of slaves held within federal territories (where the Republicans insisted slavery had never legally existed) and freed all those slaves of rebel masters who came within Union lines, whether or not it could be proved that they had been used in the service of the Confederacy. But all of these acts affected only the status of individual blacks, not the institution of slavery. By the summer of 1862 it was precisely the future of the institution itself that had to be faced. The costs of war had become too terrible to be borne without a hardening of the will to destroy the slavery that had underlain the conflict and that now helped to sustain the enemy's strength. Naked military necessity demanded that the Union deny the Confederacy, so far as possible, the labor of its slaves and that the North itself make use of blacks to fill out its armies. Since there were few Negroes to be armed in the North, the obvious course was to do everything possible to identify Union victory with freedom in the minds of Southern slaves so that they would be moved to abandon their labors and escape to Northern-held territories where as laborers or as soldiers they could aid the Union cause.

In the summer of 1862 Lincoln determined on such a course and drafted a proclamation of emancipation. Its publication was delayed until after the Union victory at Antietam in August, and it did not become effective until January 1, 1863. Even then it had almost no actual legal effect. It undertook only to free slaves within those states or parts of states that were in rebellion. It did not reach slavery in the loyal border states. Congress in July 1862 had already freed slaves of rebel owners within Union lines, and the Emancipation Proclamation obviously could not be enforced beyond those lines.

But its psychological impact was enormous. It finally had become clear that the North was fighting to restore not "the Union as it was" but a Union cleansed of slavery, that Northern triumph would mean the end of the institution, and that when the Southern states returned to the Union it would be as free states. It hardened Northern purpose and defined for foreign powers the moral contrasts of the war in ways that won sympathy and support for the North and deepened the diplomatic isolation of the Confederacy. More important still, it quickly became known to slaves throughout the South and bound their hopes to Northern victory. And finally, the impact of the proclamation made it clear that even though its language did not reach to the loyal states, slavery could not survive within a victorious North any more than in a defeated South.

By the narrowest of margins, a new state constitution ended slavery in Maryland in 1864, and the advance of Union arms through the South enforced the Emancipation Proclamation over an ever-widening area. With the surrender of the principal Confederate armies at Appomattox and Durham's Station in April 1865, slavery, as a legal institution, was nearly at an end. But its foes demanded a more complete and unassailable victory. The institution maintained a vestigial existence in Delaware, Kentucky, and Missouri; and the Emancipation Proclamation by which it had been abolished in most of the South was merely an exercise of uncertainly grounded executive war powers. A readmitted Southern state, if it retained a constitutionally sanctioned power over the institution within its borders, might well restore slavery. A constitutional amendment was the only means of extirpating slavery everywhere within the Union and of placing its revival beyond the power of any state.

In January 1865 Congress finally proposed such an amendment to the states; and the total abolition of slavery, which had been flatly renounced by the federal government as a goal at the war's beginning, now became one of the essential aims for which the war was fought to its end. The North was no longer fighting to restore the old Union but to create a new Union, in which neither slavery nor the right of secession could have any part. The amendment obtained the necessary ratifications and became a part of the Constitution in December 1865. Slavery was abolished even before the Union was restored.

CHAPTER FIVE

───

In Which North and South Debate the Role of Blacks, and the North Leaves It to the South to Decide

THE END OF CHATTEL SLAVERY was determined by the collapse of the Confederate government and the surrender of its armies. But nothing else had been decided about the future of blacks. There were four million freedmen in the midst of a destroyed and leaderless society that had been based on their labor. Almost all of them were illiterate. Most were untrained save in agricultural labor and unfamiliar with life outside the narrow ambit of the farms or plantations on which they had been owned—landless, propertyless, moneyless, unschooled in the independent management of their lives and earnings. To refit this enormous body of men and women usefully and justly into the fabric of American, and particularly of Southern, life would have been a nearly insuperable task, even given the best will and the most ample of means. And there was little of either. The South was impoverished, the North ill disposed to spend its money there. Even the bitterest foes of slavery were by no means necessarily the friends of slaves. Lincoln himself would have rid the whole country of them if he could; and their very presence was blamed for the evils of slavery, for the war, and even for their own wrongs and sufferings. Only among the old abolitionists were there men who persisted in looking beyond the end of slavery to the integration of blacks into American life as free men.

Decisions as to the new role of blacks in the South were worked out in conflict between two forces: the dominant white community of the South and the power of the victorious North, each with its own views as to what that role should be. It was Lincoln's intention and that of his successor, Andrew Johnson, that self-government should be rapidly restored to the former Confederate states. As soon as hostilities were suppressed in any state and a nucleus of citizens could be identified who were loyal to the Union and prepared to accept the war's outcome, both Presidents were willing to entrust to them the formation of a new state government. By the end of 1866 Lincoln and, after his death, Johnson had recognized reconstituted governments in all the Southern states except Texas and had welcomed their return to the Union.

These states, fresh in their recovered sovereignty, would be free to deal with the Negro as they saw fit, short only of re-enslaving him. For almost two years after the end of hostilities, Southerners who were willing to accept the formal abolition of slavery could otherwise reshape the relation of whites and blacks very much as they chose.

They had two main objectives: as quickly and inexpensively as possible to get blacks back to work and to restore such discipline over them as would reduce white fears of robbery, rape, and insurrection. Both these objectives were sought in the "Black Codes" enacted by many Southern legislatures in 1865 and 1866. That of Mississippi, though more extreme than most, exemplifies their content.

The new Mississippi constitution abolished slavery, and the various acts that made up the "Black Code" gave certain previously denied civil rights to the Negro. He could marry, own personal property, sue and be sued, and testify in person (though not by affidavit) in cases in which a Negro was involved or which concerned a crime committed against a Negro. At least nominal protection was given him by state supervision of labor and apprenticeship contracts into which he might enter. But his status remained far below that of whites. He could not, for example, vote or serve as a juror, or hold office, or testify in cases among whites. No provision was made for his education. He was entitled only to such poor relief as could be provided from a special tax levied on blacks alone. A number of acts were crimes if committed by blacks but not if by whites, and for others a different and more degrading penalty was provided for blacks. Blacks, even those with seven-eighths white blood, were forbidden to marry whites on pain of life imprisonment for both.

Special provisions of the code were aimed at stifling any black attempt at violence or insurrection. Blacks were forbidden to assemble unlawfully, to own or carry weapons, to acquire intoxicants, to preach unless licensed, and to commit "riots, routes, affrays, trespasses, malicious mischief . . . seditious speeches, insulting gestures, language, or acts, or assaults on any person, disturbance of the peace . . ." and a variety of other offenses. Moreover, all the prewar legislation defining crimes of slaves and free Negroes were made applicable to the freedmen of the postwar era. Though the effect of this last provision was unclear, it gave local authorities sanction to apply to free blacks the curfews, bans on travel, and similar provisions of the antebellum slave code.

Even more significant, however, were those provisions of the new Black Code aimed at compelling the blacks to work on the cotton plantations in a form of peonage. Any Negro not regularly employed after the second Monday of January 1866 was defined as a vagrant, and in most cases his employment had to be evidenced by a written contract. But almost no employment was open to him except farm labor. He was denied the right to own or rent land, except as incorporated towns might license him to do so. Hence he could neither operate his own farm or move to a town to look for work. Even to be employed by the job, as an independent artisan or casual laborer, required the permission of local authorities. Unless he already had an established position in a town as an artisan or domestic servant, the Negro, foreclosed from all other opportunities, was compelled to enter into a "labor contract" on the white man's terms. In no other way could he earn food or even find a place to live.

Once he had entered into a contract, formidable sanctions compelled him to fulfill it. A Negro who left his job during the term of his contract could be arrested and returned like a fugitive slave. Black children without support could be sold into apprenticeship, with preference in the purchase of their labor given to former masters. A number of other provisions of law were aimed at compelling the labor of blacks on white terms. If, for example, a Negro failed to pay the special taxes levied for the support of the indigent of his race, or was temporarily jobless, or was convicted of any of the manifold and vaguely defined offenses lumped under "vagrancy" ("insulting gestures," for example), his punishment could take the form of having his labor sold to a master for a period of time to repay the fine imposed on him.

Most other Southern states, warned by the hostile Northern reaction to the Mississippi legislation, either did not enact "Black Codes" or adopted milder statutes. South Carolina, however, was even more stringent in denying blacks the opportunity to escape from agricultural peonage by making it extremely difficult for them to gain permission to work as artisans, mechanics, or storekeepers; and Florida's vagrancy code was, if possible, even more rigorous than Mississippi's.

Carl Schurz, the liberal statesman and journalist who made an inspection tour of the South in 1865 at President Johnson's request, accurately summarized the Southern attitudes that underlay the Black Codes. He was speaking of Mississippi, but his remarks were applicable, sometimes in tempered form, to most of the South. He said that it was the view of Mississippians "that the negro exists for the special object of raising cotton, rice, and sugar *for the whites*, and that it is illegitimate for him to indulge, like other people, in the pursuit of his own happiness in his own way. Although it is admitted that he has ceased to be the property of a master, it is not admitted that he has a right to become his own master. . . . It is, indeed, not probable that a general attempt will be made to restore slavery in its old form . . . but there are systems intermediate between slavery as it formerly existed, and free labor as it existed in the north, but more nearly related to the former than the latter, *the introduction of which will be attempted. . . .*" (*Senate Executive Documents*, No. 2, 39th Congress, 1st session, pp. 21, 32, as quoted in Vernon Lane Wharton, *The Negro in Mississippi, 1865–1890*, p. 82.)

Perhaps even more significant for the long run than the active efforts of Southerners to maintain a firm control over blacks and to compel their continued service as plantation laborers was the Southern failure to provide any alternative. Even with slavery abolished, any marked improvement in the actual social and economic condition of the blacks depended on their ability to acquire land and education. There was no slightest disposition on the part of the defeated Southern states to provide either. Landowners stripped of all else clung to their acres and fought to recover the land seized by federal troops. By statute, as in Mississippi, or informally, as elsewhere, Negroes were effectively blocked from acquiring land. In the first postwar years there was neither money nor energy for the education of either white or black; but even had there been, its use for the education of Negroes would have encountered the same opposition that had made it a crime in the prewar South to teach a black to read or write. If there were to be any real release of the blacks from the prison of their situation, it would have to come from the use of Northern power and resources.

But there was little disposition in the North to seek a truly equal role for Negroes in the political, economic, and social life of the country, North or South; and Northerners might have left the South undisturbed in its management of blacks had the new governments of the Southern states not shown such an open, willful, and unrepentant determination to resume an unchanged role in the national political life. By the Black Codes and similar legislation they had expressed a resolve to maintain the enforced subservience of blacks with as little change as possible in their actual status as compared with the days of slavery. They elected to state office and to the Congress men who had been fiery secessionists, who had held high office in the Confederate government, and who had commanded rebel troops. With the freed blacks fully counted in the allocation of Congressional seats (where slaves had been counted only at three-fifths their number), Southern representation in Washington would be substantially larger than before the war and unchanged in its determination to preserve the substance if not the legal form of Southern institutions.

The Republican party and the forces in American life which it represented had come to power only by a minority vote on the eve of war. By no means did it have a secure control even over the Northern states. The return of an enlarged, unaltered, and unrepentant

Southern Congressional delegation and the casting of a larger Southern electoral vote would be likely to return the Democratic party to power and to reduce Negroes again to a peonage little distinct from slavery. Little would have been changed by the sacrifice of billions of dollars and hundreds of thousands of lives. And a restoration of Southern-dominated Democratic power could undo or reverse the economic policies put into force by the Republicans during the war, policies that looked to a rapid opening of the West, tariff protection to hasten industrial growth, a national banking policy, the early completion of a transcontinental railroad, and federal aid to agricultural and technical education. It was the moral outrage of the old abolitionists, men like Senator Charles Sumner of Massachusetts or Congressman Thaddeus Stevens of Pennsylvania, at the quick resurgence of former slaveholders and of slaveholding ideas and policies that led immediately to the Northern reassertion of control over the reconstruction of the South; but their thrust was supported by a complex of Northern interests, political and economic as well as moral.

This combination of motives led Congress to refuse to seat the Congressional delegations sent from the Southern states. By a series of acts in the spring of 1867 Congress restored military government in the South, supplanted the elected governors with Presidential appointees, and required that new state constitutions be drafted by conventions for whose members all adult males, white and black, could vote, with the suffrage denied only to unpardoned Confederates. These constitutions themselves were required to provide for Negro suffrage. A new constitutional amendment was drafted that was intended to give federal protection to the basic civil rights of all citizens, blacks included, against hostile state action; to penalize states that disfranchised blacks by reducing their Congressional representation; to guarantee the payment of the federal war debt and to assure the repudiation of the Confederate debt; and to disqualify from voting and office-holding certain classes of Confederate leaders. Ratification of this amendment by the seceded states was made a further condition of their recognition as full members of the Union.

It was unfortunate that a two-year interval had elapsed between Southern defeat and the North's undertaking to use its victory to reconstitute Southern society. The stunned and disorganized South of the summer of 1865, conscious of its utter defeat and helplessness, could not have effectively resisted major internal changes. But in the intervening two years it had recovered its organization and will and something of its pride and self-confidence. It was doubly bitter at being for a second time subjected to Northern rule.

However, submission was quiet if sullen. The conventions were called, the constitutions drafted and adopted, the new constitutional amendment (to be the Fourteenth) ratified, and one by one the Southern states were returned to their normal legal relation to the Union. The internal political revolution within the Southern states was this time a major one. The exclusion of many former Confederates from the vote and the enfranchisement of the Negro resulted in a political overturn in each of the states. Only in South Carolina did the constitutional convention or the new legislature have a majority of blacks; but in all the states political control passed to the Republican party, made up of blacks, of Northern whites ("carpetbaggers" in the derisive terminology of the time) and a large body of native whites. A few of the latter were in fact the "scalawags" they all were called—unprincipled men greedy for power and its accompanying opportunities for plunder. But most of them were men of character who had been Unionists in 1861: uplanders from the areas where there were few slaves and much hostility to slaveholders, poor whites excluded from participation in the prewar governing classes, a few men of wealth and substance who saw the future of their states in a new order. The Reconstruction governments simply reflected the fact that a majority of Southerners, taking black Southerners and white Southerners together, were opposed to the political and economic order that had governed the prewar South and that was striving to regain control.

The state constitutions prepared by the Reconstruction conventions were by no means radical or irrational. Most of them, in fact, were patterned closely after the constitutions of one or another Northern state. They did, however, markedly alter the status of blacks by allowing them the vote, by eliminating explicitly discriminatory legislation including the Black Codes of 1865 and 1866, and by providing for a system of free tax-supported schools open to all. The Reconstruction constitutions and laws did little or nothing, however, for the economic status of the freedman. Nothing was done to give him land or an opportunity to buy it or to assure him an untrammeled access to the various trades and professions. In general, the objectives of the Northern Reconstructionists were primarily political and were

in part theoretical. Once the Negro was freed and given
the vote, and the states were required by the Constitution to respect his rights as a United States citizen and
allow equality under the law, many Northern radicals
felt that blacks now had the same rights and status as
whites and must work out their own destiny for themselves.

But the day-to-day life of blacks was little affected in
any immediate way by these political and legal changes.
They enjoyed a greater security of person and family,
a slight measure of personal dignity previously unknown,
an opportunity to remove themselves from absolutely
intolerable conditions. But to break loose from the con-
fines of ignorance and poverty in which they had been
forced to live through all the generations of slavery
would require radical economic and educational changes.
Even with a more just distribution of income between
landowner and laborer, the plantation cotton culture of
the South simply could not produce enough to sustain
its laboring force at a decent level of subsistence. And
even this cotton economy would be years recovering its
prewar productivity. It would be fifteen years after the
war before the first significant stirrings of industrialization would arouse the prewar hopes for Southern manufactures. And in any event the black farm or plantation laborer had little training that would have enabled
him to find a ready place in manufacturing or even in a
more diversified and modern agriculture.

The South had never made any systematic effort at
the education even of the whole white population.
Schooling beyond the barest rudiments of literacy, and
often even that, was privately given at the expense of

parents if at all; and a very high proportion of the white population had grown up unlettered. In the disorganized society of the immediate postwar period, the massive task of educating the four million freedmen was utterly beyond the region's resources.

Any serious Northern intention to change the actual lives of the former slaves would have to be evidenced in three ways: by providing them with land on which they could use their considerable agricultural skills for their own benefit; by a massive input of Northern funds and teachers to begin the enormous task of education and vocational training; and by the willingness to use military force if necessary to protect the blacks in the exercise of their rights. Perhaps because no one realized how formidable these tasks were, perhaps because the will itself was wanting, the North did none of these things or did them only flickeringly and without lasting effect.

To give land to the freed blacks was the most immediately important and would have been the most practical measure. But the land could have come only from the confiscation and redistribution of plantation holdings. A legal basis for such action had been laid in the Confiscation Act of 1861, but this statute never commanded either Lincoln's or Johnson's support and was never seriously enforced. When peace had come and confiscation could no longer be justified as a war measure, it became doubly repugnant to the mores of that property-conscious time. During the war there had been various experiments along the Carolina coast and in Mississippi in which freedmen had the opportunity to operate for their own profit lands abandoned by Confederate owners, and they had done so successfully. But with the return of peace, even these farms had been taken from the blacks and restored to their prewar claimants, who were treated with a tenderness quite lacking in the confiscation of Loyalist estates during the Revolution. A few radicals in the North continued to agitate for expropriation measures to give lands to the blacks, and the freedmen beguiled themselves with rumors of a distribution of "forty acres and a mule" at the Christmas-tides of 1865 and 1866. There was some dalliance with the idea that blacks might be given a preferential access to free lands in the public domain, but this too came to almost nothing. There was no serious effort at any time to give the freedmen any measure of economic independence that could shore up their political freedom or compensate for their generations of unpaid labor.

A tentative effort was made at schooling. The Freedmen's Bureau, created in March 1865 to provide acutely needed food and shelter to the former slaves, many of whom had been displaced from their homes, also set up makeshift schools where it could. Approximately five thousand idealistic Northerners came South in the immediate postwar months as volunteer or missionary teachers. Tens of thousands of blacks received an unaccustomed few weeks of learning.

None of these efforts made any serious impact on the problems of Negro education. The first flush of postwar enthusiasm waned by 1870, and in spite of a continuous effort by Northern religious groups, the primary burden of education of blacks and whites alike was left to the Southern states themselves. Though the

Reconstruction constitutions of all the readmitted states contained provisions requiring the maintenance of free public schools open to all, little was done to carry this mandate into effect. There was no real conviction in most of the South that education, other than for the gentry and a small elite of professionals and managers, was a necessity even for whites. There remained among the dominant group an active conviction that the education of blacks was a positive evil, engendering dissatisfaction with their role as farm laborers, making them "uppity" and doing nothing to improve their work. The provisions of the Reconstruction constitutions reflected an imported idealism little shared among the groups rapidly returning to Southern power. But even had there been a real devotion to the goal of universal free public education, there were neither the funds nor the teachers nor the experience that could have achieved it without massive Northern aid. And even the token effort of the Freedmen's Bureau and the wave of volunteer teachers and missionaries who had followed the Northern armies had dwindled by 1870.

Progress was not wholly lacking. Painfully and slowly schools were established, teachers were found, and children were enrolled. Northern churches revived and enlarged their educational efforts among Southern blacks in the 1880s and 1890s. The colleges and secondary schools then operating provided most of the education above the elementary level available for the training of black leaders. But the effort was poorly supported financially and was able to enroll annually only a few thousand students. The primary schools, almost wholly dependent on local support, were few, miserable, and often distant and they were open usually only for a very few months or even weeks during the year. The training offered hardly went beyond the barest rudiments of literacy and arithmetic and there were almost no public high schools. Most teachers were themselves half educated at best, untrained in teaching, and wretchedly paid. Even as late as 1880 only a minority of white children of school age were actually enrolled in the South, and half or more of those enrolled were likely to be absent on any day. Education for blacks lagged far behind even this minimal achievement. Blacks were denied access to white schools throughout the South even in those states, such as Louisiana and South Carolina, whose Reconstruction constitutions forbade racial segregation. As conservative whites held or regained control of local governments they were loathe to devote to black education any but the barest minimum, if any at all, of the pitifully inadequate school funds. Indeed, the educational opportunities of blacks deteriorated in the 1870s and 1880s as Northern support at the elementary level was withdrawn and the public authorities in the South did little or nothing to replace it. As late as the end of the century the great majority of Southern Negroes were still imprisoned in illiteracy.

The third element of needed Northern support for the Negro was the use of legal and military measures to protect his rights. This reached its high mark with the ratification of the Fifteenth Amendment, prohibiting the denial of the right to vote on grounds of race, color, or previous condition of servitude. The reconstructed states had been required to provide for Negro suffrage in their new constitutions, but there was no power to prevent the rescinding of such measures after the states were readmitted to the Union and no federal authority to enforce the provisions of the state constitutions. Hence the radical Republicans pressed for a constitutional amendment that would give a permanent federal protection to black suffrage. By no means was Northern sentiment unanimously favorable to such an action. Few Northern states had granted the suffrage to blacks or were eager to do so within their own borders. Indeed the necessary ratification by three-fourths of the states was obtained in part by requiring it as a condition of readmission of the three Southern states still held outside the Union. A genuine concern for justice to Negroes and a fear that if their franchise were rescinded by state action they would be left defenseless against renewed oppression were sincere motives of many of the advocates of the new amendment. The primary concern of others was to assure the Republican party a substantial basis of loyal Southern voters.

The amendment was ratified and came into effect in 1870. Its provisions were negative rather than positive. It did not require that Negroes be allowed to vote, but merely that race, color or previous condition of servitude not be the basis for excluding them. States were left entirely free to use literacy, the payment of poll taxes, the ownership of property, or similar tests to bar from the polls a class of voters who would in fact be predominantly black.

The final Northern effort to use federal power to protect Southern blacks in the exercise of their rights came in 1875 with the long deferred passage of a Civil Rights Act which sought to implement the Fourteenth

Amendment by prohibiting racial discrimination not only by public authorities but also in hotels, inns, railroads, ships, and other places of public accommodation. This was, however, the last move of a North already weary of the Negro and his problems. It was never seriously enforced, and within less than a decade its key provisions were to be held unconstitutional by the Supreme Court.

For Southern whites Radical Reconstruction greatly complicated the problem of working out new means of controlling blacks and using them in the region's economy. They had hoped, through the Black Codes and similar legislation, to maintain their complete dominance over a race that, though legally free, had no political rights and no economic opportunity for survival except as laborers in the white man's enterprises on the white man's terms. Radical Reconstruction thwarted this plan by giving blacks nominally equal political rights, creating state governments sympathetic to them and in part dependent on their votes, and maintaining at least a token presence of federal troops to protect them. The use of blacks would have to be worked out on new terms.

The most urgent problem, in white eyes, was to keep them steadily and dependably employed at plantation labor without the necessity of compensation rising significantly above the bare subsistence level of slavery. Not only diligence was required but dependability. The peak labor demand in cotton culture came at the end of the season, when the bolls were picked and ginned. Comparable labor demands came at the harvest season of tobacco and sugar cane, when the tobacco had to be stripped, cured, and prized and the cane cut and pressed and its juices processed into molasses and sugar. It was indispensable that labor once committed at the planting season remain steadily at work through the harvest.

Wage payments severely taxed the very slender capital resources of the planter and left the worker free to leave in the midst of the growing season or to extort a higher wage under threat of quitting at cotton-picking time. And there was fear as well that fixed wages would not be an adequate way of holding workers at the labor to which in the days of slavery they had been driven by fear of punishment.

Out of these difficulties in the postwar decade a new method of using blacks was developed: sharecropping. This was a form of tenancy in which the laborer and his family were given a plot to farm which was committed to one of the commercial staples, usually cotton, less often tobacco. The tenant typically furnished nothing but his own labor, for which he received a cabin of sorts to live in, credit at a local store to cover his minimal needs while the crop was growing, the necessary seeds and tools, the use of a mule as needed, and after the harvest a share, usually one-half, of the crop. The share-cropper was not really a tenant, using his produce to pay rent, but a laborer working under the landlord's direction and receiving his wages in kind. A laborer with some means, who could supply his own plow, tools, mule, and seeds, became more genuinely a tenant with more independence and a larger share of the crop.

Sharecropping had many advantages for the landlord. He had no obligations to the tenant unless he remained to get the crop in. This bound the worker to the land throughout the growing season almost as effectively as had slavery. The incentive to produce enough to yield some cash return at the end of the year above the charges for maintenance provided a stimulus to labor more effective than slavery's threat of punishment and lessened the necessity of expensive supervision. The constant possibility of being evicted into homeless poverty lay over the sharecropper to assure his subservience. Though the tenant's freedom to leave at the end of the year made it necessary for the planter to provide a certain minimum of food, clothing, shelter, and fairness of treatment to prevent his labor force from simply melting away, this need be little more than the subsistence level of slavery, so desperate were the blacks for any employment at all. And the landlord was correspondingly free of any legal obligation to maintain his employees in sickness, infancy, or old age or to provide them with medical care or similar services.

It was well recognized that under the contracts prevailing between landlords and "tenants" only the most extraordinary diligence, skill, and luck would enable the tenant to gain anything for his year's labor above what had been advanced for his bare living. The cost to the employer was little if any more than that under slavery; nor was the black's true freedom much greater than under the bondage. His economic dependence was riveted tighter by the fact that he had to sustain himself on credit throughout the year, credit available to him only upon his landlord's guarantee and only at a designated store. The store in turn was likely to be owned in whole or in part by the landlord himself. High prices and higher credit charges levied there ground down the worker and choked the little chance of his having at year's end any substantial cash due him for the year of his life. This usually foreclosed his chance to move to new jobs or places, to buy or rent land, or enter a small business, or educate his children. A share-cropper ending the year in debt was compelled to contract with his employer for a new year, with the old debt added to the new year's burdens. Even the rare tenant with a slight balance in his favor had to contract almost immediately with one landlord or another for the new year to gain credit to buy food for his family and to have a hut to live in.

But a final boon to the planter from the sharecropping system was that it let him use white labor as well as black without violating local mores. Southern whites would not be willing to work in a hoe gang with blacks, but they would sharecrop an adjoining piece of land. This doubled the labor force on which the landowner could draw and gave him the bargaining edge he needed to hold his payments to blacks and whites alike at the margin of subsistence.

This method of using labor, however, like slavery itself, imprisoned the employer along with his employee. His lack of capital to pay cash wages or to invest in agricultural machinery compelled the landowner to continue to use labor in the sharecropping pattern. To make that system work, he had to compel his tenants to devote almost their entire energies to the cash staples. Only such crops as cotton and tobacco were acceptable security for the cash advances the planter himself needed or provided the liquidity the money-poor economy demanded. Hence there was little flexibility in the planter's ability to respond to market changes. In the face of a decline in the price of cotton, the labor system left the planter with little freedom to respond by shifting acreage from cotton to other crops or workers from cotton culture to other occupations. Indeed, almost the only course open to him was to *increase* his production of cotton, in the hope of offsetting lower prices by larger quantities, thus compounding his own difficulties and those of his region and class. Meanwhile, though the share system gave the tenant an incentive to maximize each year's production, it gave him none to preserve and increase the productivity of the plot assigned to him. Part of the price of tenancy was neglected buildings, abused work animals, leached-out and over-cropped land, and gullied and eroded fields.

Nevertheless, the sharecropping system, at whatever cost, did "work," and the black labor force was reorganized and maintained. The production of staple crops recovered and indeed soon surpassed its prewar level. A trickle of money began to flow again into the destitute region, and a slow economic recovery began.

It was not quite possible, however, for the white community to hold blacks to the nearly absolute subordination of the days of slavery. But much was accomplished toward that goal. Terrorist societies were the first resort. Hooded horsemen gave themselves ominous or noble titles—the Ku Klux Klan, the Knights of the White Camellia, the Constitutional Union Guards—and threatened blacks who dared to be self-assertive with beatings, torture, and even death. These threats were often and openly fulfilled, and the lashed and burned bodies of blacks made a public exhibition. The federal

acts of 1870 and 1871 helped to reduce this open violence, and within two or three years the klans, dis-
credited even among the better classes of whites, had
become nearly inactive. But they had already done
much of their work. What was thought to be due humility was restored to the outward aspects of the behavior of most blacks; and the less bold and the less
committed stayed fearfully away from the polls. Few
indeed had the resources or the security to assert their
rights aggressively.

Chicanery was used when violence was not dared.
Once conservative whites by diligent organization and
ruthlessness regained control of the state legislatures,
complicated systems of balloting were often adopted
that made it almost impossible for an uneducated man
to cast a valid ballot without assistance—assistance
which would be informally given the illiterate white
and denied the black. When other means failed, simple
fraud in the counting of votes was used. Through one
device or another, by the end of 1877 all the Southern
state governments had been recaptured by the conservative minority.

But their hold remained incomplete and insecure.
Negroes still sat in Congress and in the state legislatures and still held local office. The black vote, however, reduced by fraud and violence, remained a factor
of varying consequence. More extreme measures of repression were likely to bring public outcry, the intervention of the federal troops still stationed in the South,
or even the threat of further Northern intervention.
The conservative whites had returned to mastery, but
an uneasy mastery that they imagined to be threatened
daily. A complete recovery of their status could follow

only on the abandonment of Northern concern for the status of the Negro.

Politics and economics here played into white Southern hands. The scandals of the Grant administration had offended voters North and South, and many more had been turned away from the Republican party by the sharp panic of 1873 and the ensuing depression. For the first time since the Civil War, the pro-Southern Democratic party had a good chance to return to power in the election of 1876. Its Presidential candidate, Samuel Tilden, was a man of integrity and ability whose character was in marked contrast to the shabbiness of the last years of the Grant regime and who was a far more impressive figure than the unforceful Rutherford B. Hayes, the Republican nominee. Tilden indeed carried a plurality of the popular vote and what appeared to be a majority of the electoral vote.

Before conceding the election, however, Republican leaders saw a chance to retain control. There was a possibility of contesting the vote in Florida, Louisiana, and South Carolina. If the Republicans were successful in all three of these maneuvers, the victory would go to Hayes by one electoral vote. Democrats in turn hoped to claim one Oregon electoral vote on a technicality. The conflict and the charges and countercharges of corruption became so confused that Congress was unable to agree on a counting of the electoral vote. The whole matter was referred to a specially created Electoral Commission of Senators, Representatives, and Supreme Court Justices. The commission gave the victory to Hayes by a vote of 8 to 7, divided strictly on partisan lines.

Outrage at this apparent theft of an election inflamed

the Democratic party, and had the country not been
weary of war, violence might well have followed. As
it was, a basis of compromise had already been laid in
the agreement to refer the contested votes to the commission, and further compromises led to Southern acquiescence in the results.

The price of this acquiescence was a tacit agreement
to end the active Northern concern in "internal" Southern affairs. Shortly after Hayes's inauguration the few
remaining federal troops were withdrawn from the
South. Federal district attorneys in that region became
less vigilant in the prosecution of cases involving the
denial of civil and political rights to blacks. Hayes himself was earnest in his pleas for sectional reconciliation,
in his praise of Southern loyalty, in the blandness of his
hopes for quiet peace.

In this he reflected a national mood as well as an election compromise. For forty years the abolitionists and
their spiritual successors had shrilled in the national ear
their complaints about the treatment of Negroes. A
bloody and painful war had been fought. Slavery had
been ended, the franchise guaranteed to blacks by Constitutional amendment. Bored Northerners with little
love for blacks at best had had enough. What more,
they asked, do the Negroes want? We have given billions of dollars and hundreds of thousands of lives to
free them. We have extended them the vote. We have
passed laws to protect their personal rights. We have
listened to the "Negro question" for a generation.
Enough! The economy, recovering from depression,
was on the edge of explosive expansion in manufacturing, in railroads, in Western settlement. There was no

time or energy to waste in wrangling over ignorant blacks on Southern farms. Let the whites and blacks down South work it out themselves somehow and let the war at last be over.

That was the mood, and it triumphed. After 1876, it was the Southern whites who decided the fate of blacks.

CHAPTER SIX

━━━

In Which Southern Whites Restore Control of Blacks

THE YEARS FROM 1876 to 1890 were a period of exhausted truce in race relations. With Northern support withdrawn, the promised votes denied or made useless, and the hopes of educational and economic progress crushed, Southern blacks had mutely to endure the blighting of their dreams of freedom. Northern whites had turned away from the whole problem in bored frustration. Southern whites, still burdened with extreme poverty, drifted in torpor once they had dislodged the blacks from a share in political power.

In the North and West a vigorous national economy was growing with staggering speed. Thousands of miles of new railroad lines were opened annually. Gigantic iron and steel plants at Pittsburgh, Cleveland, Chicago, and other cities were roaring into the night. Within decades open prairies were converted into crowded slums. Textile mills were doubled and tripled in size and number. New coal mines were sunk. Gigantic assemblages of capital were created and applied to the development of new industrial empires.

This economic revolution created an endless demand for men for the hard labor of the new factories and railroad gangs. But in spite of the reserves of underemployed manpower, black and white, on Southern farms, this labor was drawn almost entirely from Europe and, on the West Coast, from Asia. In the 1880s, 5,300,000 immigrants came to the United States; in the depression decade of the 1890s there were 3,700,000; and in the first decade of the twentieth century these figure rose to 8,200,000. This flood continued until the outbreak of World War I and in the years 1910–1914 brought another 5,175,000. In contrast with this intake of nearly 25,000,000 European and Asian migrants, the population flow from the South to the rest of the country was relatively small, averaging only little more than 50,000 a year, of whom only about 20,000 a year were black. For every Negro brought from the South to fill the jobs created in the North by the new industrial revolution, more than thirty laborers were brought from Europe. The blacks who did move north before World War I were employed principally in personal services, as hostlers, porters, draymen, longshoremen, unskilled laborers on the railroads, coal miners, helpers in the steel mills, and common laborers generally. Almost none of them were drawn into jobs that would lead them out of unskilled labor into skilled and truly productive employment. American society made almost no use of blacks in its gigantic industrial transformation in the years from the Civil War to World War I. Like Southern whites, but at an even lower rung, they remained imprisoned in the cotton economy.

It is surprising that the hungry Northern economy would turn to so distant and alien a source for labor when a Southern surplus of less efficiently employed labor was so close at hand. In part this was due to a prejudice against black workers on the part of Northern labor and employers. In part it was because of a higher level of education and skills among the European immigrants, in part because of the greater thrust of the highly organized emigration from Europe. But principally it was because of the numbing isolation of the Southern, especially the black, rural worker, whose ignorance, poverty, and inexperience imprisoned him more effectively than actual walls and bars. And because he was still useful in the expanding cotton economy, his bosses wanted to keep him under that restraint.

In the decade and a half after the end of Reconstruction there was no such industrial transformation in the South as that which swept the North. Cotton culture reached and passed its prewar level, and by 1890 the South was producing nearly two and a half times as much cotton as in 1860. The seemingly endless world demand created a market for all that could be grown but at lower and lower prices as new areas came into cotton production here and abroad. In the continuing deflation of the 1880s and 1890s, cotton growing barely remained at the margins of solvency and generated no profits that could be used to improve its efficiency. Except for the increasingly costly use of fertilizers in desperate repair of its ravages of the earth, it went on its unchanging way, with the patterns of sharecropping ever more firmly implanted, annually depleting both the soils and the human resources of the region.

Once Negro political power had been broken and Northern support withdrawn, blacks were left so powerless in the South that for a time no further assaults on their legal position were found necessary by Southern whites. The laws supporting the vote for blacks were left impotently on the books. Many blacks remained on the electoral rolls; some voted from time to time; a very few were even elected to office.

For fifteen to twenty years after the end of Reconstruction, this anomalous situation persisted. Though sharecropping had been substituted for slavery as a means of organizing and controlling Negro labor, the economic and social condition of blacks was little changed. They continued to live at the margins of subsistence, with even less security than under slavery. Doors of opportunity were narrowly opened for a very few blacks of exceptional ability, energy, and luck; but for the great mass of the race the ways to educational or economic progress or political influence were as firmly barred as in the days before emancipation. Yet this slightly transformed peonage existed within a body of laws that presumed full Negro equality with whites in their civil, political, and economic relations. Under the menace of white violence and fraud, most unaided blacks were simply powerless to use or even to claim the rights that were theirs under law.

Four developments disturbed the truce in the 1890s. One was a slow return of economic and political vitality to the South itself. The end of Reconstruction and the re-establishment of cotton culture permitted a return to the tentative thrust toward industrial development that had been apparent in the 1850s. Railroad construction was resumed, and throughout the South the 1880s saw a budding development in cotton-mill construction.

Cigarette manufacture was born; and, along with the production of pipe and chewing tobacco, it became the center of a thriving new industry. A nascent ferment of change began to be felt in the region by the 1890s. Funds began to be devoted, in small amounts, to higher education, and the possibility of more realistic support of education generally began to emerge. The exciting prospect could be foreseen of a more fluid and more prosperous economy. The "New South," however unrealized in fact, took on reality as a hope, indeed as a confident expectation; and the role of the black in this changing society would have to be defined.

A second force was provided by the slow, very slow, formation of a small group of educated and articulate Southern Negroes who could give organization and a voice to their race. In the integrated society of slavery the religious and medical ministry to blacks was given, to the extent it was given at all, by whites; and if blacks were taught at all, they were taught by whites. The opportunity to set up any form of autonomous black organization was ruthlessly denied. Segregation and the abandonment of white responsibility, on the other hand, offered certain black opportunities. A few black schools survived Reconstruction, notably at Hampton and Atlanta, and others, such as Tuskegee, were created shortly thereafter. Aided by Northern support, they annually offered to a few thousand blacks an opportunity for education beyond elementary levels. Black teachers were trained or half trained for the few Negro schools that were opening, and a handful of blacks became physicians, lawyers, and other professionals. Negro undertakers and storekeepers began to emerge to serve an increasingly separate black community. Negro newspapers, mostly church-supported, were established in a few Southern centers.

Far more important was the emergence of separate Negro churches. In the early years of emancipation many blacks continued to attend white services, sitting in galleries or balconies, and even in some cases were admitted to membership. But they soon withdrew or were expelled and began to form their own congregations, as they had in the North long before the Civil War. These were quickly formed into or affiliated with national bodies. A National Baptist Convention of Negro churches was formed in 1880, and national Negro Methodist organizations that antedated the Civil War grew rapidly. By the late 1880s there were national, state, and local hierarchies of these churches, giving Negroes a substantial experience in organization and a national network of communication. Now unsupervised by white observers, the meetings of black congregations and their related social groups for the first time gave an opportunity for an autonomous black public opinion to form.

Though their level of instruction may often have been little if any above that of most high schools, the struggling Negro colleges at Hampton, Atlanta, Tuskegee, and elsewhere provided another group of focuses for forming and organizing black public opinion. So did the few Negro newspapers that existed in the South by the 1890s. These various organs of the black community were by no means radical or even militant. Indeed, the principal ostensible message of the black schools and churches was one of acceptance of and successful adjustment to a white-dominated society. But for the first time a self-conscious black community was beginning to emerge as an autonomous entity with its own leaders, with tentative elements of organizational structure, and with some capacity, however weak it might yet be, to exercise influence as a coherent body. White policy in the era of slavery had been firm and conscientious in choking off even the possibility of such a coalescence so that the white community would have to deal only with individual blacks and not with a black community. The mere possibility of this threat now awoke white leaders to the need of firmer and more comprehensive measures to protect white control.

A third factor was an alarming, even if tentative, renewal of Northern interest in Southern blacks that followed the return of Republicans to power in Washington in 1889. President Harrison spoke disturbingly if vaguely about Negro rights. Legislation was before Congress in 1890, misleadingly but effectively damned by Southerners as a "Force Bill," that would have reasserted a national interest in protecting the rights of black citizens. In the same year the Blair Bill, which would have provided federal aid to education in proportion to the degree of illiteracy in each state, passed the House and seemed likely to pass the Senate. Southern schools would have been the principal beneficiaries of the bill, and in deference to Southern sentiment it made no requirement for the integration of schools. But it did require an equitable distribution of funds on a per-capita basis between black and white schools if separate systems were maintained; and this was too much for many Southern white leaders. The education of blacks they saw as more dangerous than the ignorance of whites;

and in spite of their desperate need for educational funds they willingly sacrificed the possibility of improving the schooling of Southern white children to avert what they saw as the ominous threat of an educated black community. In union with other opponents, the more conservative Southern Senators succeeded in defeating the bill in the Senate. But once again they were alerted to the danger of a situation in which a legal assertion of equal rights for blacks, however ignored in practice, was allowed to remain unchanged in the statutes.

It was the Populist uprising of the 1890s, however, uniting blacks and poorer whites in an attack on the Southern political and economic establishment, that triggered the ruthless movement throughout the South to disfranchise and segregate the Negro legally. The condition of all farmers, Western and Southern, black and white, growers of wheat and of cotton, had steadily worsened in the generation following the Civil War. Deflation and the opening to rail transportation of fertile new farming areas had forced down the price of staple crops year by year. The farmers were not only becoming poorer but felt politically weaker as the cities burgeoned. In a total sense they felt every year more subservient to a growing and arrogant money power.

In the 1890s the fear and resentment of the farmers blazed out in the formation of the Populist party. After an impressive but unsuccessful campaign in 1892, it sought national and state power in 1896 by fusion with one or another existing party. Nationally the Populists united with the Democrats in support of William Jennings Bryan for President; but in the South the state Populist parties frequently fused with the Republicans and put forward joint tickets in state and local selections.

Only in North Carolina, where the Republican party had retained a considerable strength, was this union successful. But in that state the Republicans and Populists together in 1894 and 1896 elected the governor and a United States Senator and a majority of the state legislature and of the Congressional delegation, as well as local officers in many counties. Elected among them were a considerable number of Negroes, including a Congressman, ten state legislators, and many minor county and municipal officials.

In all the Southern states, whether or not there was a successful Populist-Republican fusion, the political uprisings made Negroes once more a factor in elections. The Democratic leadership found it necessary to make concessions to blacks to hold their votes. It became apparent that any serious division among whites offered power and influence to blacks. And black votes offered the chance for white dissidents to threaten the Democratic establishment. White dominance over blacks was threatened, and along with it the dominance of the new power group of manufacturers, railroad owners, bankers, businessmen, and larger planters over poor whites. The latter was perhaps the more immediate and more frightening danger. The response to both was a hardened determination not only, as in the 1870s, to drive blacks from real participation in political power but to eliminate them permanently from the electorate.

The pattern for achieving this disfranchisement had been set in Mississippi in 1890. In this state blacks were a large majority and had been an important political force. Even after the return of Southern whites to power and the withdrawal of federal troops, it was not possible to drive blacks entirely from office. Throughout the 1880s half a dozen or more Negroes remained in the state legislature, and there were enough Negro voters to make it necessary for white office-seekers to give some heed to their rights. Even this somewhat shaky white predominance could be maintained only by the open and continuous use of fraud and violence. As one of the delegates to the 1890 state constitutional convention admitted: ". . . it is no secret that there has not been a full vote and a fair count in Mississippi since 1875, that we have been preserving the ascendency of the white people by revolutionary methods. In other words we have been stuffing ballot boxes, committing perjury, and here and there in the state carrying the elections by fraud and violence." (As quoted in Vernon L. Wharton, *The Negro in Mississippi, 1865–1890*, p. 206.)

Even before the Populist uprising, revulsion against these methods and resentment by the poorer whites of the hill counties against the use of black voters as allies by wealthier whites in the plantation counties had led to a drive to find some legal means of disfranchising blacks. This drive was given urgency by the "Force Bill" being debated in Washington in 1890.

The result was a constitutional convention which met in 1890 determined to find a way to nullify the Fifteenth Amendment by devices that would stand up in court. This was achieved by a combination of poll tax, residence, and literacy requirements, coupled with a provision that any conviction for any one of a number of criminal offenses with which Negroes were frequently charged should disfranchise an otherwise eligible voter.

Even if impartially administered, these provisions would have fallen with special weight on blacks, penalizing them for having been denied the means to earn an adequate income or obtain an adequate education or acquire a permanent residence or to be dealt with equally in the criminal courts. But an impartial administration would have let some blacks vote and would have denied the vote to many poor and illiterate whites. This would in fact have been a desirable outcome in the eyes of conservative Democratic leaders, but it was politically unacceptable. Instead, the literacy test was modified by a provision that enabled a voter to qualify by proving his understanding of a provision of the Constitution read to him, a test intended to be easy for whites and impossible for blacks to pass when administered by a white registrar.

The Mississippi plan worked. Blacks were almost entirely eliminated from the voting rolls and played no further significant part in Mississippi politics for generations. Though challenged in the courts as a violation of the Fifteenth Amendment, it was sustained by the Mississippi Supreme Court and ultimately, in the case of *Williams* v. *Missisippi* in 1898, by the United States Supreme Court.

As a result, the Mississippi example was ready to hand when the other Southern states faced the threat of revived Negro political power in the 1890s, and they all used it with one modification or another. Between 1890 and 1900 almost all of the former Confederate states and a majority of the border states had amended their constitutions or adopted entirely new charters with the primary purpose of providing a legal, if indirect, method of disfranchising blacks in the face of the Fifteenth Amendment. By 1908 the roll was complete. Of the several devices used, literacy tests were the most useful. They had national sanction, as they were coming into wide use in the North to protect the older society from having to share political power with recent immigrants and were approved by Northern intellectuals and liberals. And they were marvelously flexible. The Mississippi test of "understanding," used in that state as an alternate to the literacy test, in other states was incorporated into the test itself, so that a prospective voter had to read *and* interpret a section of the Constitution selected for him by a registrar who had the unreviewed and final authority to accept or reject the interpretation. A white sharecropper with a second-grade education might well pass such a test when a black graduate of Harvard would fail.

But the cautious whites did not rely on literacy tests alone. Property qualifications were experimented with in several states, and in nearly all a poll tax was required. The primary impact of this tax came not from its amount, which was relatively low, but from the requirement that it be paid long in advance of the election, even so long as one or two years, and that a receipt be retained and presented if demanded at the voting booth. Moreover, most states did little or nothing to collect the tax or to notify those liable that it was due. The result was that most black—and many white—potential voters lost their franchise through inattention or ignorance of the requirement. Conviction of any one of a number of petty crimes was made an added ground of disqualification in most states.

In order to assure, as in Mississippi, that the laws did not disfranchise poor or illiterate whites, they were skewed in two ways. One, already referred to, was by the discriminatory application of the "understanding" clause of the literacy tests. The other was by the use of "grandfather clauses." This device originated in Louisiana but was widely copied in other Southern states. It allowed those who had voted prior to the enfranchisement of the blacks, or who had been Confederate soldiers, and their descendants to register without compliance with the literacy tests. By this means, the literacy test was in fact made a test for blacks only.

To make assurance not only doubly but triply sure, yet two more devices were added. In North Carolina, for example, the state legislature, securely under white Democratic control, was given the power to elect local officials from slates nominated by the local parties. This gave the government of every county into the hands of its white Democratic citizens, even though there might be a majority of black or Republican or Populist voters.

Most crushing of all was the white primary. The Populist party collapsed after its defeat in 1896, and the Republican party was made impotent by the disfranchisement of most of its black supporters. After 1900 the Southern states were one-party commonwealths. General elections became formalities, and all meaningful decisions were made in the Democratic primaries. In the Southern view, the Democratic party was a private organization, free to define its membership without reference to the Fifteenth Amendment. In almost every Southern state, the party explicitly excluded Negroes as such, whatever their means or education, from voting in its primaries. An occasional intrepid Negro might risk personal violence, might have so advanced an education that the most prejudiced registrar could not deny his literacy, might have the means and foresight to meet any property qualification and to pay his poll tax long in advance and keep his receipt, might have the persistence to get himself registered in an election office that regularly closed as he appeared or was out of forms when he applied. But all that he would have for this great and perilous effort would be the empty opportunity to vote in a meaningless general election as one of a handful of his race too small to have any hope of affecting its results. It is little wonder that apathy was added to all the other limitations on the black franchise.

This systematic program of disfranchisement was remarkably successful. By 1900 the black vote was almost completely eliminated from one end of the South to the other and along with it much of the poorer white vote that might, as in Populist days, unite on economic issues with the blacks to challenge the dominant white classes. So thoroughly did the system work that even a generation later when hundreds of thousands of blacks were clearly literate and well informed and easily able to pay poll taxes, almost none voted. Only fragmentary statistics are available, but they are remarkable. In Louisiana 130,344 Negroes were registered in 1896. The new constitution was adopted in 1897 and by 1900 the Negro registration was reduced to 5,320; and by 1904 this figure was only 1,718. Total elimination of black voters had been achieved in eight Louisiana parishes (the equivalent of counties) by 1900. This number increased year by year until, in 1928, forty-two of the state's sixty-four parishes had absolutely no black voters. In Alabama by 1908 there were only 3,742 Negro registrants among 121,159 male Negroes over twenty-one and literate. The number of adult literate Negroes, male and female, had risen to 269,847 in 1920, but fewer than 3,500 blacks voted in the following decade. Similarly, in Mississippi, which had nearly 300,000 adult literate Negroes in 1920, fewer than 1,000 voted in the following decade. In that decade, fewer than 5 percent of potential Negro voters actually voted even in relatively liberal Virginia. (The foregoing statistics are from Paul Lewinson, *Race, Class, and Party*, Appendix II.) And it should be remembered that almost all of this handful of votes were wasted in general elections with foregone outcomes, and almost none of them were in the Democratic primaries, in which the only meaningful contests took place.

Equally remarkable was the success of this group of schemes in withstanding legal attack. Eventually the Supreme Court held that "grandfather clauses" could not be permanently available to exempt whites and whites only from literacy tests; and in the 1940s explicit provisions barring Negroes from Democratic primaries were finally voided. But the essential parts of the scheme remained effective until the 1960s. As a result, from 1900 to the 1960s the Negro was simply eliminated from Southern politics. And not until World War II were there enough Negro voters in the Northern states to provide a black voice in the political life of the nation. For two long generations whites were entirely free to make unilateral political decisions affecting blacks without the necessity of taking black voters into account.

During these same decades there was not even the

moral pressure from Northern whites that in the decades before 1890 had imposed on the white supremacists at least the necessity of equivocation. Millions of immigrants, few of whom were literate in English or knowledgeable about American life, were pouring into Northern and Midwestern cities in the years from 1890 to 1914, frightening the guardians of traditional American values. Among the Brahmins of New England, who had been the principal, if tepid, defenders of Negro rights, there developed a sudden concern for the problem of excluding ignorant and "different" masses from the vote as a means of preserving the power of a proper elite. And with this new concern came a tolerance, even an approval, of the Southerners' method of solving that problem.

The Spanish-American War contributed greatly to Northern acquiescence in white Southern racial policy. The common patriotism of Northerners and Southerners and their fighting side by side warmed fraternal feelings. But much more important was the surge of imperial ambition that led the United States to take dominion over the Philippines, Guam, and Puerto Rico and to establish a protectorate over Cuba. It was necessary to develop a rationalization for the right of a dominant race to control the political life and future of a less advanced people without their consent. The attitudes of a McKinley or a Roosevelt toward their "little brown brothers" in the Philippines were very like those of a Henry Grady or a Charles Brantley Aycock or other spokesmen of the New South toward their black "charges." British, German, and French apologists for colonial expansion had already worked out the requisite justifications—the racial and cultural superiority of the white race and the right and indeed duty of that race to take over the rule of lesser breeds without the law. The dominant white leaders, men like Theodore Roosevelt and Elihu Root, bursting with a newly heightened and jingoistic nationalism, were eager to join the company of the admired British in their Kiplingesque role as benign rulers and exploiters of weaker peoples. They saw the Southern white in a new and romantic coloring, as the long-suffering, responsible, and conscientious guardian of Anglo-Saxon civilization, maintaining it with firmness and dignity amid the childlike and incompetent blacks who played the role of "natives" in this self-flattering drama.

With Negroes left politically impotent and their former protectors in the North converted to the support of white supremacy, Southern whites by 1900 had been almost completely freed to organize and control the black labor force as they wished. For nearly half a century this authority was all but unlimited, threatened neither by black power nor by serious white concern. It was used with energy and persistence to establish a comprehensive system of both legal and extra-legal controls that wiped out most of the black gains from the Civil War and Reconstruction beyond the bare fact of emancipation itself. Raeford Logan has called these years at the turn of the century "the nadir"; and truly the blacks had been returned to a state little better than slavery.

CHAPTER SEVEN

In Which Control of the Powerless Blacks Is Perfected

THE FIRST STEP in the forging of the new controls over Negroes was to achieve a complete segregation of black and white societies except for the minimal contact necessary to make use of black labor. Blacks and whites had been intimately associated in the antebellum South, even though the association was one of master and servant. Blacks lived in or near white houses, traveled with whites when they traveled at all, were taught —if taught at all—by white teachers, treated by white doctors, often preached to by white ministers. In spite of a general separation of whites and blacks, the few Northern Negroes with money enough to eat at good restaurants or stay at hotels or travel on trains or ships were usually able to enjoy the same accommodations as whites. And for the first fifteen years after the Civil War this was often true as well of the few Southern Negroes with means to use such facilities at all. They too, if bold enough, might drink at saloons and eat at restaurants and ride on trains and streetcars patronized by whites.

But this changed sharply in the 1890s and after. The gradual increase in the number of blacks who could afford such amenities angered whites into restrictive legislation, which they were free to adopt after the disfranchisement of blacks. This freedom was affirmed by the Supreme Court in the *Civil Rights Cases* of 1883, in which it was held that the Fourteenth Amendment did not give the federal government power to protect Negroes against private discrimination, as by hotels or railroads, and in the famous case of *Plessy* v. *Ferguson* (1896), in which the Court declared that even segregation by state law was constitutional so long as the separate accommodations were, or were asserted to be, equal.

Seizing upon this opportunity, every Southern and border state by 1910 had enacted laws separating blacks and whites in almost every public contact in which they might otherwise have been associated as equals. These statutes began with transportation, requiring separate cars on railroads, separate areas on ships, separate seating on streetcars, and separate waiting rooms in stations. Segregation in accommodations followed, with blacks denied access to "white" hotels, restaurants, and saloons. Segregation in schools—already a fact wherever blacks had schools at all—was embodied in law. In some states, segregation was prescribed even in employment, with bans against blacks and whites using the same working areas or restrooms.

By 1910 this legal structure was complete in the Southern states, and blacks were almost entirely cut off from association with whites except as their laborers and servitors. No matter how dignified his bearing, how immaculate his person, how polished his manner, every

black was crowded into separate and actually grossly unequal accommodations whenever he sought most sorts of
service outside his own home. Jim Crow had been fixed
into law and had become rigid in a way never known
before.

The next step was to deal with the problem of education. In the decades prior to 1900 the Southern states
made no serious effort at state support of public education. Locally supported elementary schools for whites
were general by the end of the century, but at a pitifully
low level. They were wretchedly housed, were open
for only a few months or even weeks each year, were
poorly taught by ill-prepared and worse-paid teachers,
and were attended irregularly by children who were
subject to no compulsory attendance law. Negro elementary schools for the most part existed only where the
initiative of Negro families created them, and they were
maintained largely by volunteer Negro contributions
with minimal public support. With very few exceptions,
public high schools existed only for whites and only in
cities. Few students, white or black, went past elementary school. Most of the whites who did attended private academies, and the few Negroes who pursued a
further education were likely to do so at one of the
Negro colleges, most of whose students were in fact at
the high-school or even elementary-school level. The
total educational contribution of the states was so pitifully small that discrimination in its distribution was not
an important issue before 1900.

But by the turn of the century there was a growing
dissatisfaction among white farmers and workmen, unable to afford private schooling and demanding publicly

supported education for their children. Educational campaigns, financed in part by Northern philanthropists, were mounted throughout the South to win taxpayer backing for a state-supported public school system in every state.

This immediately raised the question of Negro education. Voters who were grudgingly willing to be taxed for the education of their own or their white neighbors' children were flatly unwilling to be taxed to give black children an education that would, they feared, only make them unfit or unwilling to be exploited as farm labor. The success of the efforts to provide Southern white children with educational benefits they so desperately needed depended on devising means to exclude Southern black children from those benefits. Hence it was that Southern liberals, educational leaders, progressive men remembered until today as generous and democratic reformers dedicated to the welfare of children and the poor—men like Charles Brantley Aycock of North Carolina—were applying themselves in the early years of the century to plotting the exclusion of blacks from equal educational opportunity.

Negroes could not be totally ignored in the educational revival of the early twentieth century. Even the slack judicial attention to the civil-rights aspects of the Fourteenth Amendment which then prevailed would have demanded at least some ostensible equity in the division of funds between white and black schools. The principal technique of evasion was to provide that state funds should be distributed among the counties on a population or school enrollment basis, without regard to race, leaving local authorities to apply the funds to individual schools as they might judge the educational needs of the county required. This had a doubly discriminatory effect. Local authorities, remote from the attention of the federal courts, did not hesitate to hold to a pittance the allocation of state funds to Negro schools, following the patterns already established in the allocation of local funds. This meant that in the black-belt counties a minority, even a quite small minority, of white children would receive the benefit of a state appropriation made on an equal per-capita basis that included blacks as well as whites. White students in predominantly black counties thus had not only an overwhelming advantage over black students but a marked advantage over the white students of predominantly white counties. It meant further that discrimination between whites and blacks was greatest in precisely those states and counties in which most blacks were concentrated. This discrimination was further intensified in the pre-World War I years by the fact that the greatly increased school funds provided in that period still came predominantly from local sources, free from even the feeble assurances of equitable treatment provided in the state appropriation acts.

The Southern educational renaissance of the early twentieth century radically improved white education. Though the financial support of Southern white schools remained far below that in other parts of the country, it was several times as high by 1915 as it had been at the beginning of the century. But ominously significant was the dramatic widening of the gap between white and black schooling. Almost equal in the poverty they both experienced in the 1880s and 1890s, they had become markedly different in 1915. Throughout the region by the latter date the expenditure per student was six to twelve times as high for white students as for black students and in some localities the ratio was even higher. Negro school buildings were poorer—usually unheated and unpainted one-room cabins without electricity or running water. Negro schools had shorter terms, fewer teachers, and larger classes, averaging nearly twice as large as white classes. The most complete statistics by race were kept in South Carolina. In that state by 1915 the value of school property was $32.11 per white child and $2.57 per black child, a ratio of more than twelve to one. Annual expenditures on current school operation were $13.98 per white child and $1.13 per black child. Black teachers received on the average $112.31 a year for teaching sixty-four children; white teachers received $383.39 for teaching thirty-six children. The average white school term was twice as long as the average Negro school term. By every measure of expenditure on elementary education in South Carolina, the funds devoted to the "separate but equal" black schools were, on a per-student basis, about one-twelfth the expenditure on white schools.

The further and shocking fact was that this discrimination had markedly grown in the previous fifteen years. In 1900, for example, expenditures per capita for white schools had been only four or five times that of black schools, instead of ten or twelve. The average length of term for black schools had actually declined, from seventy-five days to sixty-seven, while that for white schools had increased over the same period from 105 days to 133.

Though there are not equally detailed figures by race from all Southern states, it is clear that there were comparable developments in all. In North Carolina, for example, the state in 1900 was spending half again as much per child on the education of whites as on that of blacks; in 1915, three to four times as much. In Virginia counties with a large Negro population, expenditures for teachers' salaries in 1915 were about nine times as high per white child as per black child. Georgia in 1915 spent six times as much on the education of each white child as on that of each black child. In the lower South educational progress came later, and the discrimination against blacks was, if possible, even more severe.

The sharpening of educational discrimination in the pre-World War I years was in part the consequence of poverty and general racial antipathy. Unable to provide even meagerly for all, the dominant whites provided first for their own. But to an even greater degree, the discrimination was a matter of deliberate social policy. It was intended on the one hand to prepare young whites to take part in the New South and indeed the new nation, in which commerce and industry and urban life were expanding. And it was intended on the other hand to assure that Negroes, denied other opportunity, would remain available for rural labor at bare subsistence. These objectives were plainly avowed, particularly in the debates that were carried on in those years throughout the South over the adoption of compulsory school-attendance laws. Over and over orators pointed out that with black children in schools and not in the cotton fields the cotton crop would stand unpicked; that educated Negroes would move to other occupations and by passing

the literacy tests undo the disfranchisement just
achieved. A small mill owner quoted in Louis R. Harlan's *Separate and Unequal* (p. 125) summed up the attitude of most Southern employers on the education of
Negroes: "It looks quite plain to me that it is necessary to
have educated people fill higher positions, and . . . a
large number of illiterate people who perform the labors
of the country. I believe that this was ordained from the
beginning." Many employers, especially in the cotton
mills, in fact felt precisely the same way about the education of the children of white laborers at public expense; but the whites could vote and hence could protect
the educational opportunities of their children. The
blacks could not. Disfranchised by Southerners, abandoned by Northerners, they were nearly helpless to
gain an education for their children that would open
for them any door of opportunity into the burgeoning
economy of the twentieth century.

The discriminatory use of education as an instrument
of economic policy was even clearer at levels beyond
elementary school. Prior to 1900 secondary education
in the South had been almost entirely college preparatory
and almost entirely private. Throughout that region the
public high school was a concept of the twentieth century and was almost entirely for whites. Even in the relatively advanced Atlantic coast states from Virginia
through Georgia there were only 2,130 black high-
school students as late as 1916, and half of those were in
the one state of Virginia. In that year in all of North
Carolina there were only nineteen black high-school
students. A city as large as Atlanta had no Negro high
school even in 1917. Almost no Southern educational

leader, even among the most "liberal," was willing to advocate spending tax money to give blacks any education beyond the rudiments of literacy and agricultural and domestic skills that would enable them to serve their employers better. None argued for giving blacks the kind of education that might help free them from the peonage in which they were held.

Yet in those same years, public white high schools were being established throughout the South in a great rush of construction and organization—and for the obverse reason: A higher level of education was essential to enter the new economic life that was developing. It was deliberate policy to give the key that opened the door to this new opportunity to white youths and to deny it to blacks.

Negro colleges were established but supported only with pitifully meager funds and only upon the understanding that the training they offered (most of it actually at pre-college levels) would be only "industrial education," intended to train blacks to perform more efficiently the agricultural and domestic labor for which they were destined, or to become teachers to train other blacks in the same skills. Even the few Negro leaders with any power to affect the situation recognized that black education in the South, if it were permitted at all, would be permitted as a means to fit the black more effectively into his role as an exploited worker in the lower levels of the economy, not to give him the means to escape that role. Near the end of his life Booker T. Washington pointed out: "We are trying to instil into the Negro mind that if education does not make the Negro humble, simple, and of service to the community, then it will not be encouraged."

Disfranchisement, segregation, and denial of education did not exhaust the official measures taken by the Southern states to assure Negro subservience. Denial of equal justice was another. The vast machinery of the law was a white instrument for the orderly enforcement of white will. The statutes were enacted by legislatures in which, after 1900, blacks almost never sat and voted on by representatives whom disfranchisement had left with no black constituency they were required to respect. Every judge was white, from the state supreme courts to the lowest magistrates. Every sheriff and policemen was white. Almost every lawyer was white. In all the South there were only a handful of black lawyers, most of them poorly trained, little respected, and without influence in the white courts. Even the jurors were all white.

The instruments of the law were not only all white. They were an interlocking network of power, suffused by a common determination to maintain the suppression of blacks. Southern judges were elected and faced re-election at the end of fixed terms. They sat in no life-tenured independence of local sentiment, and they were by no means isolated from politics. The lawyers who pleaded before them and with whom they were united in an easy camaraderie were nearly all politically ambitious. In the Southern atmosphere of those years as later nothing could so fatally injure a political career as the charge of "nigger lover"; and nothing could so completely deny a lawyer the hope of affluent clients as a suspicion of undue concern for the rights of the poor, and especially the black poor, in their controversies with men of property. Sheriffs and their deputies, jailers and wardens, city police were likely to come from poorer white families and to reflect the prejudices of those whose racial hostilities had been exacerbated by poverty and insecurity. The secrecy of the jury room was no protection to a juror who might vote to convict a white man or acquit a black one in a case in which racial issues were involved or to sustain a black man in a suit against a white over rent or wages or crop shares.

The law was the white man's law. It was negligent and inattentive to crimes and controversies among blacks, so that respectable Negroes had little protection against rowdy criminals of their own race. It was almost impossible to obtain even an arrest, much less a conviction, of a white man for violence against a Negro. Especially was this true if the violence was deliberately racial and intended to avenge any black activity displeasing to the community. Even in civil actions the courts afforded no real hearing to a Negro who believed himself defrauded by a white man of his wages or his share of crops.

The indifference of the courts to Negro rights and the unresponsiveness of elected officers to the interests of a race without a vote left Southern blacks at the extralegal mercy of the white community. A rigid pattern of race relations, with a "place" to which the black was to be confined, embodied all the law's discrimination but went beyond it. The most important element in this pattern was the ruthless confinement of blacks to unpleasant and low-paid jobs. Manufacturing grew intensively in the South in the decade before World War I, but blacks were barred from the factories except as sweepers and unskilled laborers. Railroads expanded rapidly as well, but here too Negroes were confined to laborious or servile jobs—as track laborers, shop helpers, porters, and firemen. (Later, when automatic stoking equipment eased the fireman's job, that too became a "white" assignment.) The governmental jobs that had often been open to blacks in the generation after the Civil War were steadily closed as the century ended. In the years of slavery and for long thereafter many, if indeed not most, Southern artisans were black, including highly skilled carpenters, tailors, bricklayers, and painters. These jobs too were increasingly closed to blacks as they began to function as competitors rather than servants of whites. Even jobs with overtones of personal service, such as barbering, were changed from "Negro jobs" to "white jobs" and black barbers and hairdressers were left with none but black customers.

The Negro who wanted to become an independent farmer or start a business of his own faced formidable obstacles. White custom narrowed his chances of buying farm land, or even of obtaining it on a cash rental. He had to be "good" enough and highly enough regarded—and the land poor enough and isolated enough —for the white community to give its tacit consent to the purchase. Since he would find little willingness of a bank to lend money on a mortgage, and would have had scant hope of saving the purchase price from his cropper's shares, he was even then faced with the need to find a friendly seller who would allow him to pay over a term of years. If he sought to open a store or any other business in town, he was faced with the same near impossibility of obtaining capital from a black community that did not have it or from a white community that would not lend it.

The object of this confinement of blacks to share-cropping and farm labor and to the hardest and lowest-paid city jobs was in part to save the better-paying jobs for whites. Fecund white rural families were pouring forth generation after generation from the small farms across the South. They moved into the towns hungry for jobs and took over for themselves whole categories of work that had formerly been performed by Negroes. Their unwillingness to share jobs with blacks or work alongside them forced employers to operate all-white plants. But perhaps an even more important object was to assure a continued adequate supply of farm labor at subsistence rates of pay to meet the continually rising demand for cotton and other Southern staples. The panicky hostility with which Southern whites confronted recruiters who sought to entice Southern blacks to come North as strike-breakers or low-paid workers is evidence of their intense dependence on the system of peonage that provided cheap labor for their fields.

Economic, social, and political motives for suppressing blacks were inextricably interwoven. The exploitative position of Southern whites would be threatened by black progress in any of these areas. Economic opportunity that would enable blacks to escape the cotton fields would not only threaten the labor supply but would give them an economic basis for social and political independence. Education and other social advancement would make it harder to deny blacks the vote and economic development. Any black recapture of political strength would threaten the security of the systems of social exclusion and economic exploitation. The system was a whole, enforced as a whole. Its success depended on its complete, firm, unchanging application. Blacks might be left free to hope for more fairness and consistency in the administration of the system, and individual blacks might be allowed to strive, through diligence and subservience, to win preferred positions within the system; but no hope that the system itself might ever be overthrown could be allowed to spur black ambition and resentment. The success of the system depended instead on resigned acquiescence.

A variety of extra-legal methods were employed to buttress the legal system and make its enforcement complete. One was a system of racial etiquette, pervasive throughout Southern life. One of its functions was to reduce racial friction by providing a generally understood pattern to govern all racial contacts. But its principal purpose was to emphasize to both races, continually and at every point, the less than human status of the Negro and the innate and unquestionable superiority of the white. Most aspects of life were governed by this code, beginning with forms of address. No adult white was called by his bare first name by any black. If he were well known from childhood to an older black, or he had to be distinguished from his father or his brothers, he might be "Mr. Bob" rather than "Mr. Jones," but never "Bob." Similarly, no black was ever addressed as "Mr.," "Mrs.," or "Miss." An elderly and respected Negro might be "Uncle George" or "Aunt Sarah." A physician or high-school principal might be "Dr. Smith" or in the latter case "Professor Smith"; a minister could be "Reverend Jones," an attorney "Lawyer Johnson"; but most Negroes, whatever their age or dignity, were plain "Jack" or "Mary," even to white youths and children.

A black came to the back door, not the front door, of a white man's house. He was received, if at all, in the kitchen or porch, not in the living room. Except as an extraordinary act of condescension to a favored black who was ill or elderly, whites did not enter black homes. Segregation was extended by custom to areas the law did not reach. In no circumstance did blacks and whites mingle as equals in any social sense. They might meet in an office on business, and might hunt or fish together, or work together in a field or tobacco barn or at a cotton gin. Out of doors, black and white men might eat together from their lunch pails or from a meal cooked over a campfire, but they never ate together indoors or sat together at a table. Churches and private social activities were as rigidly segregated by custom as were schools and parks and trains and restaurants by law.

In all the contacts that were permitted between the races, Negroes were expected to behave with subservience and humility. In smaller towns they were expected to step off the sidewalk in the street to allow whites to pass. In offices and stores they were to stand aside until the business of all whites had been attended to. They spoke to whites with averted eyes and in respectful tones. Any words or attitudes that a white might think "fresh" or impudent or "uppity" might bring violent punishment.

The extralegal code was particularly severe in all

relations between black men and white women. The utmost caution was required of black men to avoid any conceivable affront to a white woman or any remotest suggestion that they existed as members of opposite sexes of the same species. Any act, however innocent, of a black man that offended or frightened a white woman, however irrational or hysterical, might quite literally cost him his life. In a hundred other ways the code separated and subordinated blacks, but in none so ruthlessly as this.

The code of etiquette had many practical benefits for whites in assuring them the pleasures of deference and flattery, in avoiding having to await their turn in offices and stores, and in general in asserting their privileged position. But the greater importance was symbolical and educational. Whites and blacks alike lived from birth in a context in which every incident, every relationship, every attitude taught blacks that they were different and inferior and whites that they were different and superior, with the result that nearly all whites and most blacks accepted their respective statuses as a fixed and inescapable condition, rooted in the immutable nature of things.

Such a conditioning of the young of both races was essential to the success of the whole system. Any people subjected to the exploitation endured by blacks would have risen in destructive, even if suicidal, rage if they had not been unremittingly impressed from childhood with the naturalness and inevitability of their lot, if they had not been taught hour by hour and day by day by their every experience throughout life that blackness was an irremovable stamp of inferiority and that no

Negro could escape the particular social role assigned by his race. If ever Negroes could come generally to believe that their position in society was no fixed and inevitable consequence of race but was one deliberately forced upon them by white men in order to exploit their labor more efficiently, there would be a torrent of outrage—a torrent in which the system itself would have collapsed.

But the ceaseless training of whites was equally essential. Once the system of subordinating and exploiting blacks lost the legal sanction of slavery, its maintenance more than ever required the unremitting determination of whites. If in the Southern white mind blacks had been among the "all men" the Declaration said were created equal—or the "all men" their religion taught were brothers—it would not have been possible without intolerable psychic stress to have kept them imprisoned in the degradation the system required. It was no easy matter to instill the necessary attitudes in white youths while at the same time earnestly indoctrinating them with the precepts of the Declaration of Independence and of Christianity.

Yet the effort succeeded. No Americans were more ardently patriotic or more fervidly religious than Southern whites, who grew up suffused with emotions about democracy and brotherhood and untroubled by the omission of blacks from the compass of these beliefs. This could be achieved only by a life experience in which *at every point* the difference and inferiority of blacks were taken for granted as inevitable. Even minor exceptions to this universal pattern, however innocuous in themselves, were exceedingly dangerous as calling into question the rationality and inevitability of the whole. No Southerner would really object to a clean and well-behaved Negro, such as those who nursed his children and prepared his meals, riding in the same railroad car— except for the questions raised: If a Negro, by meeting reasonable standards, could escape the bonds of race in a railroad car, why not in a school? In a voting booth? On a job? In a courtroom? The crack would open that might widen into the collapse of the whole structure.

So tense was the effort to preserve the integrity of this entire system that it was supported at every point not only by a legal structure dedicated to white supremacy but by extra-legal violence as well. Any Southern Negro in the late nineteenth or early twentieth century well understood that any effort to assert his dignity or independence might be construed by whites as insolence or "uppitiness" and was likely to lead to a beating. Any effort to organize a concerted black opposition and, even more certainly, any real or fancied molestation of a white woman was likely to bring not a beating but a lynching. Nor was the use of violence confined to specific suspected individuals. In such race riots as those at Wilmington, North Carolina, in 1898 and Atlanta in 1906, mobs of whites poured through whole Negro areas burning, beating, and shooting indiscriminately in order to intimidate the entire community.

These incidents of violence were not the infrequent or accidental or unrelated deeds of individual brutal men. Near the turn of the century lynchings were an almost daily occurrence—reaching a high of more than 250 in a year. Throughout the pre-World War I decades, the average number of lynchings never fell below two to three a week. Perhaps even more important than their number was their community acceptance. They were the expected sequel to any extraordinary challenge to white supremacy or to any alleged assault on a white woman. In the face of a charge of rape, it would require great courage and quick action by local authorities, including often a call for military support, to prevent a lynching. And any local official so obstinate in thwarting a mob would be likely to have ended his own political career.

Though the better educated and more liberal Southern whites deplored lynchings with increasing embarrassment, and though the actual participants were likely to be poor and ignorant, mob violence was tacitly accepted and often even openly supported by articulate and responsible white spokesmen. Many newspapers invited lynchings by their inflammatory reporting of alleged crimes by Negroes, and a number actually condoned such violence as necessary to the protection of Southern womanhood. No state political leaders took or tried to take effective executive or legislative action to stop lynching, and Southern representatives in Congress unanimously and consistently opposed legislation to make lynching a federal crime. Some Southern spokesmen supported the practice of lynching even while conceding that its victims might often be innocent, on the ground that the desired deterrent effect on Negroes was the same whether or not those who were lynched were guilty of the crimes for which they were pursued.

And in this view they were probably correct. Lynching probably did little to deter rape, the crime against which it was most often ostensibly directed, since its perpetrators were probably beyond rational deterrence. Indeed, by feeding a helpless fury against whites, lynching may well have provoked far more blind crimes of violence than it prevented. But there can be no doubt that the menace of the lynch mob ground down the Negro race. Fear walked with every Negro boy and man all the days of his life, fear that bent his head and stilled his tongue, that silenced his complaint of the cheating landowner and the brutal sheriff, that brought mute acceptance of the long and oppressive labor barely keeping a family alive, of the denial of schools, the segregation of trains and buses, the exclusion from the franchise and the jury box—indeed the whole relegation of blacks to a subhuman status. White violence, North and South, including the lynching mob itself, was no aberration of individual madness or sadism but a considered and necessary, if distasteful, element in the system of white control. It was indeed the ultimate basis of that system—the final answer to any black appeal to law or reason or justice.

In one respect, however, the system of white control created in the pre-World War I years differed radically from that of the pre-Civil War era. In the earlier decades whites feared beyond almost anything else any opportunity for blacks to meet, confer, or establish any sort of organization among themselves. But in the decades between Reconstruction and World War I an organized black social structure with recognized leaders and spokesmen had grown up. And now the whites had learned to use that structure and those leaders as instruments for the easier control of the black community. Black educational leaders were heavily dependent on white philanthropy for support of their institutions and for their own positions. Black business and professional men were dependent in other ways on the favor or at least the tolerance of the white community. The way out of poverty and helplessness for the ambitious Negro was to win white approval; and the way to influence in the black community was to be able to gain protection and concessions for the community from whites. Hence a reciprocal relationship grew up: The more effectively a black leader could influence his community to acquiesce in a subordinate role and to be diligent, subservient, honest, and undemanding, the more he was rewarded by personal status and the more concessions he could get from whites in the form of donations to Negro institutions and protection from or mitigation of the more brutal and lawless means of white control. Conversely, the more prestige he acquired from this status and the more evident his influence with white sources of money and power, the more effective his leadership among the Negroes. The black community and the white community each conferred on the successful black leader means and status with which he could enlarge his influence in the other. The role of such leaders in the early twentieth century was not unlike that of inmate bosses in a prison camp. They were an exceptionally effective channel for conveying white viewpoints and standards and white power through every part of the black community.

Booker T. Washington was the archetypical black leader within this framework, exercising enormous influence on both races and obtaining from white political leaders and philanthropists important boons for Southern Negroes. At the same time, acting both directly and through a wide hierarchy of lesser black leaders dependent on him, he successfully asserted a policy of Negro acceptance of a subordinate role, foreswearing social and political goals, and directing economic ambition into channels useful to the white community. But smaller replicas of Washington existed in every state and community and in every Negro institution throughout the South. Many of the abler of these leaders, and notably Washington himself, had tacit long-range goals that were far more radical, looking toward ultimate black equality. Washington and some of his colleagues viewed their acceptance of subordination and humility as a part of a body of tactics necessary in a long campaign to win eventual freedom. But at the same time they were an indispensable lubricant to the white system, perhaps helping to make it more tolerable to blacks and certainly making it easier and more profitable to whites.

On the eve of World War I, the new system of white control had reached its peak of effectiveness, and it provided a much more efficient and profitable method of exploiting black labor in commercial agriculture than had slavery. Output per man-hour of black labor in cotton production was substantially higher than before emancipation. Sharecropping made the Negro's own meager income dependent on his productivity and got more work out of him than could any form of discipline under slavery. The educational opportunities offered to blacks, minimal though they were, no doubt further increased their productivity. At the same time, the cost of black labor was probably less. Only an unusual worker in an unusual year could hope to gain more than the subsistence that had formerly been given all slaves. And the freedom of the planter from the burden of support of the elderly and invalid and from the necessity of tie-ing up capital in the purchase of slaves probably actually significantly lowered his man-hour labor cost in constant dollars.

The greater autonomy of black groups and the slightly greater freedom of individual Negroes proba-bly eased rather than made more difficult the problem of white control in the South. Black leaders won their positions and used their influence in achieving mutual accommodation within the system rather than in attack-ing the system itself, and in doing so they facilitated white control. Ambitious and dissatisfied Negroes were free to move from the South, draining radical dissent of its potential leadership. In the freer North such men usually found personal advancement more rewarding than race leadership. The minor concessions to individ-ual status and mobility made Negro life in the early twentieth-century South barely more tolerable than slavery and provided a margin above the total despair that might have driven blacks to blind and massive revolt.

But perhaps the greatest advantage of all was that the new system, by avoiding the name and legal forms of slavery, became more readily acceptable to white con-sciences, North and South alike. The destruction of slav-ery had come not because blacks had been able to rise and overthrow it but because it was no longer tolerable in the white world of the mid-nineteenth century. Even in the South itself there had always been a substantial white minority hostile to slavery. But the system of disfranchised and segregated peonage worked out by the early 1900s was acceptable to almost all whites. Its legal formulas were solemnly considered by the courts and found to conform to the Constitution, including the Thirteenth, Fourteenth, and Fifteenth Amendments. Northern whites, themselves fearing the vote in the hands of an immigrant flood from Eastern and Southern Europe and seduced by the imperial vision of white over-lordship over the colored races of the world, viewed with sympathy the Southern-white effort to maintain racial supremacy. Even relatively liberal Northerners were likely to hail the final solution of the Southern race problem under what they persuaded themselves was a benign regime of guided and controlled freedom moving under white leadership toward a carefully gradual im-provement of the black condition. And in the South, where once there were patrician liberals to regret slav-ery and poor whites to hate it, there were now left al-most no whites at all who would question the basic system of white control of blacks. The utmost stretch of Southern white liberalism was softly to deplore the ugliest and most lawless forms of violence and to miti-gate in small and personal ways the harsher sufferings endured by individual blacks.

In the South, after all the long decades of war and controversy, an uneasy interracial peace reigned over the desert of black hopes.

CHAPTER EIGHT

═══════════

In Which War Provides New Uses for Blacks

.

WITH THE COMING OF World War I, whites found a new use for blacks. In the preceding forty years Northern capitalists had filled their factories, dug their mines, built and operated their railroads with labor imported from Europe. The annual migration between 1880 and 1915 was always more than half a million a year and in peak years more than a million. Italians, Poles, Hungarians, Czechs, Slovaks, Greeks, and Jews poured into the industrial cities of the North and Middle West and Scandinavians into the farmlands. This flood entirely dwarfed the African migration that had met the comparable needs of colonial America for labor. With the outbreak of war in Europe in 1914 this flow was immediately and almost totally halted, and indeed tens of thousands of immigrants not yet naturalized returned to Europe to serve in the armies of their homelands. At the same time war demands burdened railroads and put factories and mines on double shifts. And once the United States itself entered the war some three million young men were taken from their jobs by the armed services.

This combination of factors created a severe, even a desperate, labor shortage in Northern cities, one so desperate indeed that employers were willing to turn to that long neglected resource, Southern Negroes. Factories that had never before employed a black opened their doors to them. Labor agents combed the South recruiting workers. Northern railroads enticed employees by the thousand with free transportation. Up the Atlantic coast to New York and Philadelphia they poured and in even larger numbers up the Mississippi Valley and out through the Middle West to Chicago, Detroit, and Cleveland.

Their migration was sped by the boll weevil, which in the early years of the war moved east and north from Texas destroying the cotton crop as it went. In many areas of the black belt, especially in the lower Mississippi Valley, the cotton crops of 1915 and 1916 were catastrophic failures. Though the price of cotton soared and planters in unaffected regions became wealthy, in many parts of the South no work was left for sharecroppers and no money in the landlords' pockets to finance them. If black labor was drawn to the Northern factory it was often driven from the Southern farm.

No one knows quite how many blacks were caught up in the surges of population movement between 1915 and 1920. By the census of 1920, there were 1,581,000 blacks living outside the South, an increase since 1910 of 335,000. About one-third of the growth was caused by natural increase, but nearly a quarter of a million were migrants from the South. This figure was after a sharp postwar ebb and flow in which thousands of blacks, let off at the end of the wartime boom or replaced by returning white soldiers, had gone home again to the South. At the peak of the northward tide, in 1918 and 1919, contemporary observers estimated the migration at a million. Though this figure was probably exaggerated, hundreds of thousands of blacks were dislodged from the plantation economy in which they had been imprisoned. And the quarter of a million migrants who remained, concentrated in a few localities and industries, deeply affected the character of the Northern and Midwestern cities in which they were gathered and impelled Northern whites to devise policies for the use and control of blacks that increasingly resembled those of the South.

Though the size of the migration had grown with startling suddenness, the flow of Negroes northward was nothing new. From the late 1870s on there had been a constant trickle into Northern and Midwestern cities. The principal earlier limitations on this migration had been fear and ignorance. In part these were reduced by the easier railroad connections and through services to the North which had been established by the early 1900s. But they had been overcome principally by the courage of earlier adventurers who had moved north, established themselves in urban homes and jobs, and paved the way for their friends and former neighbors to join them. By 1910 increasing thousands of Southern blacks had friends and relatives in Northern cities who could inform and reassure them about conditions in those distant and frightening centers and who could shelter them on arrival and help them find homes and jobs. As a result, even before the stimulus of the war, the northward migration was steadily mounting.

The blacks who had already established themselves in Northern cities before 1914 were used primarily as common laborers or in domestic and personal service. The men were porters, cleaners, draymen, and longshoremen. The luckier ones were waiters in clubs, restaurants, hotels, ships, or dining cars. The women were maids, cooks, charwomen, and laundresses. Few, men or women, worked in factories; none, save as porters, cleaners, or charwomen, in stores or offices. Far fewer than in Southern cities were able to gain entry into the better organized skilled trades as carpenters, painters, smiths, masons, or plumbers. The very absence of large segregated communities in the North meant that there were fewer black professionals and businessmen than in the South: fewer ministers and teachers, equally few or fewer doctors and lawyers, fewer storekeepers and undertakers. In many ways the range and variety of employments open to the Northern black before World War I were even smaller than those open to blacks in Southern cities.

But there were compensations. Jobs, even though less skilled, were likely to pay better; and a man might make more as a laborer in Chicago than as a minister or teacher in Memphis. Living quarters were poor enough but certainly better than plantation cabins or Southern urban alley hovels. Blacks tended to cluster together in all Northern cities, but there was hardly a ghetto in a contemporary sense. Even in neighborhoods where blacks were concentrated, a majority of the residents were still likely to be white. More important was the fact that schools were open and unsegregated, and the children of migrants had educational opportunities inconceivable in the South. And most important of all, there was the simple air of freedom: to sit where one pleased in a streetcar, to be addressed as "Mr.," to live without the fear of lynching.

The freedom of the Northern urban Negro was not created by the concern or liking or respect of Northern whites; it arose rather from their inattention. There were few blacks; they were an unregarded minority, granted no access to the privileged centers of Northern society but not large enough or disturbing enough to rouse whites to any special effort to deny them routine legal rights. In the interstices of indifference blacks found their small freedoms.

The new migrants of the war years were put to new uses. Stockyards, foundries, steel mills, railroad repair yards and track crews absorbed tens of thousands of immigrants. The clothing industry made use of thousands of women. Hundreds of others took lower-level clerical jobs in the large mail-order houses in Chicago—an exception to their general exclusion from office work. The traditional occupations in which blacks had been used in the North, as laborers, longshoremen, and draymen and in various forms of domestic and personal service, continued, of course, to absorb the majority of the new migrants; but the dramatic development was their entry into industrial employment.

A special use to which white employers put blacks was strike-breaking. Ignorant of the issues, desperate for work, habituated to deference and loyalty to white bosses, blacks were an ideal weapon against unions that

had made no effort to organize and protect them and
that indeed had often excluded them from membership
and from employment. This use had gone back to the
late 1890s, when Negroes were repeatedly used to break
strikes in the coal mines of West Virginia, Kentucky,
and Illinois. Steel mills and foundries in the St. Louis
area were the scene of other strike-breaking episodes.
Blacks were, in fact, used far less frequently than whites
as strike-breakers; but their use attracted greater attention and hence had greater importance. It fired racial
hatred among displaced white workers and their union
fellows. With this came further estrangement between
blacks and unions. But perhaps most important was the
fact that it gave blacks their first opening into a number
of occupations.

The decade produced the first really major shift in
the use of blacks in the economy since the seventeenth-
century importation of slaves to work the Chesapeake
tobacco fields. Three-quarters of a million Negroes were
removed from the force of agricultural laborers and
nearly 300,000 more from personal service, the two
traditional black occupations. Twenty thousand became
janitors and ten thousand merchants. Twenty-five thousand more joined the labor force of railroads. All told
170,000 more entered trade and transportation in one
occupation or another. Four hundred thousand were
drawn into manufacturing and mechanical pursuits, as
mechanics, coal miners, workers in oil fields, fertilizer
and chemical factories, blast furnaces, shipyards, and
rolling mills. A hundred thousand were added to iron
and steel mills alone, tripling black employment. Even
Southern cotton mills and tobacco factories absorbed

an additional thirty thousand. By 1920 about two million Negroes were employed in other than agriculture and personal and domestic service, an increase in one decade of three-quarters of a million.

This massive occupational shift involved also geographic shifts—not only a migration from the South to the North and Midwest, but a concentration of blacks in the cities, both Northern and Southern, in which they were employed in their new occupations. The migration of blacks from the Southern states had an added impact because of its concentration in a few states and cities. More than three migrants out of four went to six states: New York, Pennsylvania, Ohio, Illinois, Michigan, and Missouri. And within those states they were almost entirely gathered in New York, Philadelphia, Cleveland, Cincinnati, Chicago, Detroit, and St. Louis. Though the proportion of Negroes in the total population even of those cities remained small in 1920, there were for the first time in Northern cities substantial and rapidly growing black communities.

The indifference and inattention that had enabled earlier and smaller black communities to enjoy an ignored freedom were ended in those cities by the migration. The white community, having reached a decision to employ hundreds of thousands of blacks in urban industry, was compelled to make concomitant decisions as to how they would be housed, educated, and provided with social services, what their political status would be, and how they would be related to the white community.

The most important of these decisions related to housing. Prior to 1915, the Negro community in all

Northern cities had tended to cluster in areas of black concentration, but these were small and not sharply defined and were rarely wholly black. Most of them were unattractive areas in which to live, near stock-yards or factories or railroad yards or red-light districts. They were already overcrowded and could absorb few more residents. At the time of the black migration of the cities, masses of whites were being absorbed as well, moving like the blacks from farms to the promise of urban jobs. Many indeed were poor white farmers from the weevil-infested areas of the South, driven out by the same plague that had spurred the blacks. This white migration from the South was in fact larger in absolute numbers than the black migration, and much of it came to the same cities to meet the same labor shortage. During the war years scarcities of men and materials made the construction of new housing difficult; and black and white migrants were forced to compete for the limited housing supply available.

Tense hostility arose from this competition. Areas predominantly or largely black quickly became wholly black, but there was strong white opposition to the expansion of the black community into new areas. Threats, physical assaults, and bombings were the cruder and more direct methods used. Pressure of real-estate brokers was a subtler but at least equally effective method. Though zoning ordinances based overtly on race and intended legally to confine Negroes to ghettos were held unconstitutional, city authority could be used in less direct ways to keep blacks out of white areas. In better-to-do areas, real-estate covenants among groups of property owners provided a means of barring the sale or rental of property to blacks which the courts of the time were willing to enforce.

In spite of the intensity of the drive to confine the new migrants to the small traditionally black areas of Northern cities, the effort was inevitably unsuccessful. A flood so large could not be so narrowly contained. Areas adjacent to the original Negro areas in Harlem, Southside Chicago, the north-central wards of Philadelphia, and comparable ghettos elsewhere overflowed, and black settlers occupied the decaying and unattractive margins of the central cities. The white efforts at confinement were, however, successful in another and most important way. The black areas were enlarged, but they were much more sharply defined. Black areas became wholly black. Negroes who had been scattered in predominantly white areas were pressed back toward the ghettos. Large black communities were formed that were more completely segregated than any in the South. In these areas overcrowding was intense, housing conditions were very poor, and former patterns of social organization were disrupted. Both the pathology and the strengths of the Northern black ghetto were shaped.

If Northern employers were eager to recruit blacks as a new source of unskilled and semiskilled labor willing to work for low pay, white employees were determined to confine blacks to the least desirable jobs. Trade-union exclusiveness was the principal instrument used. Many unions, including the railroad brotherhoods, overtly and explicitly excluded Negroes. Others, like the machinists' union, accomplished the same systematic exclusion by secret rituals. Most other craft unions, even though they might not formally bar Negroes, in fact excluded them almost totally by requirements of long apprenticeship, sponsorship by present members, and similar qualifications. Blacks were able to gain anything approaching equal membership only in unions representing unskilled or semiskilled labor, like longshoremen, hod carriers, or miners. These were unions compelled to accept blacks or be overwhelmed by the competition of unorganized black labor. In the more desirable among the unorganized occupations, it was employers who excluded blacks on the ground that white fellow employees would resent their presence and quit, or that the public whom they might service as clerks, salesmen or saleswomen, ticket sellers, etc., would not be willing to deal with them.

An employment barrier was erected in Northern cities that confined blacks almost as exclusively as in the South to unskilled labor and domestic and personal service. The principal difference was that heavy, ill-paid, and relatively unskilled jobs in industry had replaced those in agriculture. Occupational practices and union demands barred black promotion even in occupations to which they were admitted. Black track workers could not become foremen; black dining-car waiters could not become stewards; black hod carriers could not become masons. The smaller and less completely segregated black communities in the North did not at first offer even the slender opportunities open to better educated blacks in the South to serve as ministers, teachers, lawyers, doctors, dentists, storekeepers, barbers, or cosmeticians.

Public service, at least in agencies of the federal government, had been one of the few desirable occupations open to blacks. An occasional position of dignity, such as that of Register of Deeds of the District of Columbia, had traditionally been reserved for Negroes; and the few who applied and qualified for more usual federal positions found that race, though it might impede, did not bar their appointment. In part because of the Southern prejudices of President Woodrow Wilson and the Democrats who had come with him to power in 1913, but in part also because of the heavy movement of Negroes to Washington and their increasing entry in federal jobs, the government itself adopted a policy of segregation. Blacks were separated from whites in government cafeterias, in restrooms, and frequently in working spaces. With rare exceptions, appointment or promotion to professional and executive and even to secretarial and higher clerical positions was closed. Washington, though under direct federal control, became one of the most segregated of American cities.

Another governmental decision had to be made about the use of Negroes in the armed forces. It had been the initial decision of the Union in the Civil War to use none, thinking them unfit for fighting and fearing to arm them. Moral pressure and manpower needs forced a reversal of this policy and ultimately tens of thousands of Negroes were enlisted in the Union Army. They were used largely as labor and supply troops, but thousands served well in actual combat. In the decades after the war a number of troops of Negro cavalry were maintained on the frontier and served well in the Indian wars. Negroes were again used in combat in the Spanish war of 1898.

There was no question that blacks would be inducted into the armed services in World War I. There was a half century of precedent, manpower needs were acute, and white sentiment would never have permitted black exemption from the universal draft that was then established. But their use was carefully limited. The Marine Corps took no blacks; the Navy accepted them only as messmen and servants. The Army, in contrast, accepted blacks freely, but segregated them in black units commanded by white officers. And most of these were assigned to noncombat service, largely in the Quartermaster Corps as laborers, truck drivers, mechanics, stevedores, warehousemen and the like. The general white policy was to make use of blacks to help fight the war, but to do so in ways that reinforced rather than denied the conception of them as different, inferior, and not fit to serve as equal men.

Having walled off their increasing black population in residential and occupational ghettos, Northern whites had next to consider educational policy toward them. Save in the border areas, such as Maryland, Delaware, the District of Columbia, West Virginia, Missouri, Kansas, and Oklahoma, there was no legal segregation of Northern schools. Nor, in the early years of the century, were black communities sufficiently large or concentrated to produce extensive *de facto* segregation. This changed with the migration of the war years. The widening of solid black neighborhoods left many elementary schools wholly or almost wholly black and a number of high schools predominantly so. And new educational problems were created by the influx of children who were uneducated or had been half educated in the feeble Negro schools of the South. Black schools became distinct and segregated institutions in the ghetto areas and they came to have distinct problems. A high proportion of their students, because of inadequate earlier training in the South and poor home situations, were from one to five grades below the normal for their age and had great difficulty with their classwork. Though Negroes from literate homes trained from the beginning in integrated Northern schools had previously presented no special educational problems, black students and black schools now came to have a poor reputation among white teachers and educational administrators. The more experienced teachers whose seniority gave them a choice avoided ghetto schools. Those who could not too often approached their students in the conviction that it was useless to attempt to give black youths a sound conventional education and that one must expect boredom and poor performance. Blacks schools were physically poor because their buildings were in old sections of each city and hence were themselves old. Administrators came to share the pessimism of teachers about the educability of blacks and were slow to provide black schools with books, equipment, or funds comparable to those provided white schools.

High schools in large Northern cities were more likely to have a racially mixed student body, but segregation within the school was likely to be more complete than in the elementary school as white students withdrew from social contact with blacks. Few black students were thought of by their teachers as potential college students or given the encouragement and guidance offered their comparably able white classmates.

For all its increasingly grave shortcomings, the education offered blacks in the North at the elementary and high-school level was much superior to that in the South. At least they could go to school for full terms and could continue for as many grades as their will and competence led them to attempt. And they could be taught by professionally trained (if frequently hostile or indifferent) teachers in at least minimally adequate buildings with at least minimally adequate materials.

But in the field of higher education the situation was even worse than in the South. The small number of Northern Negroes and their nominal opportunity to attend white colleges freed Northern states of any sense of special responsibility for the higher education of blacks. Wilberforce and Lincoln were almost the only Northern colleges intended for blacks, and only a very few others, such as Oberlin, encouraged their attendance. Many Northern colleges openly or tacitly barred blacks; admissions tests, high costs, and hostile pressures kept attendance at others to the barest minimum. Most Northern Negroes who wanted a college education had to go to the inferior state or church schools for blacks in the South to get it. The exclusion of black scholars from faculties and research opportunities in the North was even more complete; and the most erudite men of learning, such as W. E. B. Du Bois, though they might, in the face of great obstacles, be trained for their professions in Northern universities, had to go to Southern institutions to practice them.

By the 1920s it was clear that Northerners as well as Southerners had shaped the educational opportunities offered blacks into patterns that led not toward equality but toward subordination.

The patterns of exclusion and subordination extended into other and less formal areas as well. State law did not, as in the South, require segregation in trains, street-cars, theaters, restaurants, and places of public assembly; indeed in a number of states civil-rights acts forbade such exclusion of blacks. But it happened nevertheless. In earlier days, when it had been a rare black indeed who lived in a Northern city and had the means and inclination to eat in one of the better restaurants, his infrequent presence might be tolerated. But by 1920 the hundreds of thousands of migrants had created pressure on all manner of facilities, leading to uncoordinated but effective action to bar them from many situations. A Negro living in Chicago or New York could sit where he pleased in a streetcar and be served in his turn in a post office; but he would not be welcome in a better hotel or restaurant or in the better seats in a theater. And the wall of social exclusion that barred him from any form of intimate contact with whites was in fact far more complete than in the South itself. The process had been begun that would lead away from an integral society in which blacks played a suppressed and subordinate role toward separate societies of blacks and whites cut off from any but formal contact.

Violence was in less regular use than in the South as a means of enforcing black subordination, and the instruments of the law were less systematically employed to that end. But whenever blacks began to press against whites, competing for jobs and living space and recreational facilities, the violence was there, ready to be used.

In Springfield, Illinois, in 1908, in East St. Louis in 1917, and elsewhere in the North there were race riots in which dozens of blacks were killed and hundreds injured and in which Negro homes were burned, bombed, or wrecked. The most serious of these riots occurred in Chicago in July and August 1919. In nearly a week of bloodshed fifteen whites and twenty-three blacks were killed and 537 of both races injured. Whole Negro neighborhoods were burned. In all of these cases the violence proceeded from working-class whites who felt threatened by black pressures against their jobs and homes and who were quite ready to use extreme violence to confine blacks to narrow residential and occupational ghettos.

But the violence was not confined to momentary extremes in major riots. In the two years preceding the 1919 Chicago riot there had been twenty-four bombings of Negro homes by whites resisting the entry of blacks into previously all-white neighborhoods in that city. Blacks when first introduced into any new plant as employees were very likely to be roughed up, and black strike-breakers were in real danger. As in the South, there was a strong antiblack bias on the part of the police, who notoriously treated blacks harshly and almost equally notoriously were lax in arresting whites who assaulted blacks and in protecting the black community generally. It was indeed the refusal of a white policeman to arrest white youths who had stoned and drowned a Negro boy on a "white" beach that precipitated the Chicago riot.

By the early 1920s the Northern cities that had received the bulk of the black migration from the South in the previous decade had shaped a system of using and controlling blacks that closely paralleled that of the South. As in the Southern states, the black labor force was reserved for heavy, unpleasant, and ill-paid jobs and was denied skilled or supervisory employment. Again as in the South, education at the elementary level had become, though to a lesser degree, both segregated and inferior. Access to opportunities for higher education was even more severely restricted than in the South. Housing was better, but more completely segregated. Justice was less openly and flagrantly biased; the courts were less completely at the disposal of whites in their disputes with blacks and less completely closed to blacks seeking justice in individual cases. But in matters of social policy as distinguished from individual property rights, Northern courts as well as Southern, appellate courts as well as trial courts, found ways to avoid applying the Constitution to defend Negro rights and emasculated state civil-rights laws in application. The police forces, and behind the police forces the mobs and the bullies, were almost as completely dedicated to the use of force for the preservation of white supremacy as in the South. The Negro's "place" was less subservient, though more distant, in the North; but law and lawlessness alike were as ready as in the South to keep him in it.

The Northern system for the control and use of blacks could, however, rely less fully than that of the South on the authority of the state. The people of the Northern states were hesitant formally to legislate the controls they were quite ready to apply in practice. White Southerners might not fear to live near, work with, and mingle in superficial amiability with blacks, knowing how totally society and the state itself were ready to protect them from equality. The more fragile instruments of white supremacy in the North prompted whites to keep blacks at a greater distance. By 1920 the ghettos were more exclusive and more distant, the employment more segregated, social contact more rare than in the South. Black and white communities lived farther apart, physically and psychologically; and the daily contact of blacks and whites became less frequent and more impersonal.

Even though the patterns of Northern racist control that had been formed by 1920 were further hardened in the twenties, the northward migration began to open the way to serious breaks in the rigor and completeness of white dominance. The flow of people by no means stopped with the war's end. The new immigration legislation permanently checked the flow of laborers from Europe that had been halted by the war. The industrial boom of the 1920s had to look to rural blacks as a principal source for the mass of needed urban workers.

In the 1920s the net black migration into New York, New Jersey, and Michigan roughly tripled that of the previous decade and there were major increases in the flow into Pennsylvania and into Ohio and other Midwestern states. California for the first time received a substantial number of black immigrants. All told, the net Negro movement to the North, Midwest, and Far West in the 1920s totaled about three-quarters of a million, or more than half again as many as in the previous decade. The principal flow was up the East Coast, from Virginia, the Carolinas, and Georgia, while the exodus from the lower Mississippi Valley continued at a slackened pace. This reflected the eastward movement of the boll-weevil infestation, which reached the Atlantic in the early 1920s, and the decline of cotton culture in the seaboard states in the face of Western competition. After adding the natural increase of the black communities already in the North, the nonwhite population of the Northeast and Midwest increased by about a million between 1920 and 1930, bringing the total to more than 2.4 million, of whom 1.4 million had been born in the South.

The black population of the Northern states was almost wholly urban and was concentrated in a few cities. By 1930, New York had a black population of 328,000, Chicago of 234,000, Philadelphia of 220,000, Washington of 132,000, and Detroit of 120,000. Its occupational make-up had changed relatively little in the 1920s. Labor-union opposition and traditional prejudice continued to exclude Negro workers, North and South, from skilled trades and clerical and supervisory jobs. Factory employment increased, especially in the automobile industry, and offered somewhat more nearly equal opportunities to blacks than employment in the railroads, stockyards, and steel mills, which had been the principal new possibilities for the earlier migrants. Improving educational levels brought more blacks into teaching and civil-service positions in which color discrimination was less rigid. But the invisible walls isolating Negroes from the more rewarding job opportunities of the booming economy were nearly as impenetrable as those confining them to the deteriorating and ever more densely overpopulated black ghettos.

The real change, however, and the real threat to white control came not from the occasional opportunity Northern blacks had to participate in general public affairs but rather precisely from the ever more complete segregation and isolation of the Northern black community. The northward flow of blacks was also a cityward flow. For the first time in the history of blacks in the United States there arose large, self-contained, urban black communities. The stimulus of urban life, with its tensions, its variety, its easy communication, aroused black self-consciousness as never before. There had, of course, been blacks in cities from the earliest days of urban society in the United States; but never before had they been congregated in such numbers and in such isolation as to constitute autonomous communities.

One result was the rise of black professional and business classes, repeating the pattern of Southern towns and cities. Black-owned stores, restaurants, night clubs, barber and beauty shops arose to serve the new communities, black ministers achieved prominence in leading their congregations, and black doctors and lawyers found a practice among them. Because segregation was less complete occupationally than in the South, these infant industries and professions were less sheltered from white competition. Thousands of small white-owned stores and petty businesses sought Negro trade in Harlem and the other newly enlarged black communities, often to the exclusion of black businessmen. Almost all of the principals and most of the teachers in black ghetto schools were white. But there were some compensations. A black lawyer would find more active competition for Harlem clients than in the South; but

CHAPTER EIGHT

he would not be so completely handicapped by prejudice against him in the courts. Poor as they were by white standards, there was far more money in Northern black communities than Southern, and those who served such communities had a greater opportunity to gain means and power. The civil service, federal, state, and local, was open to Negroes, at least at its lower levels; and there was a chance both to make a living in white-collar public jobs and to acquire some sophistication and influence in the processes of government.

Most important, the black ghetto of the Northern cities provided for the first time an environment in which black leadership could rise and be sustained without depending on white acceptance. A Chicago *Defender* or New York *Amsterdam News* could assert black rights vigorously and attack white authority without risking its existence. A black lawyer could be outspoken without destroying his little role before the courts. Sustained only by his own congregation, a black minister could afford to be militant. The accumulation in one place of so many Negroes with more than ordinary drive and curiosity and with more education than was possible in the South made possible a genuine literary flourishing in Harlem. Black writers and musicians became organs of black self-awareness.

And blacks were able to become a political force again, for the first time since the post-Civil War years. Though Northern states had adopted literacy tests, aimed more at foreigners than at blacks, they were fairly administered and blacks with education could pass them. It was to the interest of the city political machines to register and use black voters as allies against the reformers of city government, with the result that Negro residents of Northern cities were sought for rather than excluded from political activity. The better to cultivate the black vote, the dominant political machines recognized—and rewarded—black political leaders.

Even as late as 1930 Negroes were still weak as a political force and were exploited by urban political machines. They had come to dominate a Congressional district in Chicago and one in New York, though not yet to elect a representative who would militantly challenge white control. Numerous assembly districts and city wards were under black control. The Negro vote was one to be wooed in the larger Northern cities. Though it did not yet have the kind of power that could challenge white racial policy at any level, federal, state or local, that vote by the late 1920s did have the kind of power that could win petty favors at city hall or the courthouse, that could provide some protection from police brutality, that could get some civil-service jobs. And a framework had been created for black political participation that could be filled out to the dimensions of a major force by the further Negro migrations that came during and after World War II.

The most important shaping of the black community, however, came from its writers. There had been spokesmen for the black community before: Frederick Douglass, Booker T. Washington, W. E. B. Du Bois. But Washington expressed white men's views of the Negro and Douglass and Du Bois were assimilated intellectually into the white community. It was largely to the white community and in its style that they wrote and spoke, however vigorously they voiced black views. A black literature read by blacks and building up a black racial self-consciousness was a product primarily of the remarkable literary flowering of Harlem in the 1920s, when writers such as Claude McKay, Contee Cullen, Langston Hughes, Walter White, and James Weldon Johnson first won serious national attention. In that same decade Negro music and life-style became a focus of emulation and participation by whites as well as blacks. For the first time, blacks came to be appreciated and to appreciate themselves as the creators of a lively, exciting, and important culture.

The actual gains of the period 1915–1930 were small; rather it was a time in which most elements of Southern patterns for the use and control of blacks were established in the North. But the creation of compact, urban black communities able to vote and free of the more brutal Southern suppression of speech and organization laid the basis for future attacks on the system. Here were the votes that in time would send black representatives to Washington and compel white representatives to listen with respect. Here were the voices that in time would spur both black determination and white conscience.

CHAPTER NINE

━━━━━

In Which a Depression and a New Deal Redefine the Uses of Blacks

IN THE EARLY 1930s the American economy had little use for men, black or white. Factories closed and stores stood empty. The produce of farms went for less than the cost of seed and fertilizer or went unsold altogether. The land emptied itself of useless farmers, whose labor had no more market than the crops they grew. Okies and Arkies by the tens of thousands migrated in despair from hopeless farms to hopeless cities or to a burdened California. Unemployed men lived in shacks jerry-built of discarded boxes and tar paper and hungered for the thin soup of the relief lines.

In this misery the most miserable were the blacks. Having been drawn to Northern cities as a labor reserve to be used in those industries and jobs for which whites could not be found and at wages below white acceptance, blacks were the first to be discarded when jobs were reduced and when whites were abundantly available for any work at any pay. Unemployment rose to disastrous levels among urban blacks, and tens of thousands of them were forced to return to Southern farms where they could scratch food from the soil to avoid actual starvation.

The calamity fell heavily on most Americans. It fell with special weight on blacks because it came at a time when the national administration was as blind to the human status of Negroes as at any time since emancipation. President Herbert Hoover was himself a man of kindly impulse but of singular racial insensitivity. For the first time in decades the Republican party under his candidacy had carried several Southern states in 1928, and perhaps he envisioned a Southern strategy that would unite his support among the farmers and townsmen of the Middle and Far West and the rural Northeast with that of white Southerners to crush the Democratic machines of Northern cities. In any event, he made even more rigid the racial segregation in federal employment and ignored the black elements in the Republican party in the Southern states. When Negro Gold Star mothers were invited to France as guests of the United States government, what might have been a gracious gesture was made an insult by their being sent in separate and inferior accommodations—not even their having suffered the loss of their sons in the nation's service having qualified them in the government's eyes with a right to equal treatment. When the Republican party showed its still effective appeal to the black voter by electing from Chicago the first black Congressman of the century, the White House's response was to insult him by long withholding and finally only grudgingly extending an invitation to his wife to have tea with the wives of other Congressmen.

Federal indifference and the actual hostility of Southern leaders and of many officials in other regions left the blacks of the Depression years in the most deprived and desperate position they had occupied since 1865. Indeed hunger, homelessness, and insecurity eroded their lives more deeply in 1932 than in 1832.

It was by no means apparent in its early years that the New Deal of President Franklin D. Roosevelt would set in train a series of developments that would ultimately revolutionize the position of blacks in American society. On the contrary, because the New Deal brought the federal government into intimate involvement in phases of American life that had previously been controlled only by private arrangements, it gave official sanction to aspects of segregation and inequality that had hitherto been informal and unofficial. When, for example, in the later stages of the New Deal, the federal government began to finance the construction of low-cost housing and to guarantee mortgages on private dwellings, it gave formal recognition to residential segregation. Public-housing developments were all white or all black. Appraisers determining the size of the mortgage the government would guarantee on a private house or apartment building were officially instructed to consider the racial homogeneity and stability of the neighborhood in which it was located. Restrictive covenants to enforce such stability and homogeneity were considered as making the property insurable at a higher value and were often insisted on.

Similarly, and even earlier, the National Recovery Administration in its approval and enforcement of industry codes for the self-regulation of the economy gave official sanction to local patterns of discrimination in employment, including lower wage rates for black employees. Though no formal racial differentials were included in wage rates on federal work relief projects, there were sharp differentials by region, by size of community, and by type of work done. This had, and was intended to have, the result of fixing the level of relief payments to Southern agricultural workers at levels below the minimum payments for marginal farm labor. The local authorities who administered the WPA were less concerned that black field hands have enough to eat than that the planters' opportunity to exploit the distress of the times by getting their farm work done at minimum cost should not be interfered with. Even in admission to relief employment in many Southern localities there was a marked discrimination in favor of whites. Destitute blacks were likely to be enrolled only after all or most whites seeking such employment had been cared for. And throughout the South employment on clerical and other white-collar projects and on those using skilled labor was reserved for whites. Black men were assigned to labor projects, ditch digging and road building; black women to projects in which they worked as charwomen or in similar forms of service.

The most serious impact upon blacks, however, came from the New Deal's agricultural policy. Faced with mountains of unsalable surplus cotton, wheat, and other basic crops, the administration's first emergency action was to plow under a third of crops in the field in 1933. This drastic step was followed up by a program to take acreage out of staple crop production and to provide support for the prices of crops grown on the remaining land. This was to be achieved by payments to farmers for lands held out of use, as well as price supports conditioned on a reduction of acreage by the benefited farmers.

But to withdraw land from use was to withdraw men from use. A small independent landowner could cut his cotton acreage and use the land and time he freed to grow uncontrolled crops. But a planter farming his extensive acres through the use of sharecroppers could be rid of the croppers entirely when he removed from cultivation the land they had worked. Share tenancy is not practical for the production of other than staple commercial crops like cotton and tobacco that are not perishable or consumable and that command a ready and known commercial value. Agricultural diversification and conservation practices that removed land from intensive cultivation were very sound in terms of general regional development, but they cut deeply into the need for agricultural field labor and cut off tens of thousands of sharecroppers from the little income they had.

Indeed, the thrust of the whole New Deal was to restore the existing economy to effective operation and to protect every individual's prior stake in it. The land-owning farmer was assured an income. The depositors' bank accounts were guaranteed. The investor was assured an honest securities market. Credit was made more easily available to land-owning farmers, the real-estate developer, and the homeowner or purchaser. The industrial worker was protected in his right to join a union, and the union in turn in its right to represent employees, to strike, and to negotiate union or closed-shop agreements. Through Social Security, industrial employees

CHAPTER NINE

age and, through minimum-wage laws, a floor under
income.

But these measures benefited only those who already had a status in the economy as property owners or
industrial and commercial employees. Federal housing
loans meant nothing to a black worker who could not
dream of buying a house, or federal deposit insurance to
one with no money in the bank. The protection of the
Labor Relations Act was worthless to domestic servants,
agricultural workers, and unskilled laborers whose occupations could not be successfully organized, and yet
these jobs embraced the overwhelming majority of black
workers. Agricultural and domestic workers were also
specifically excluded from Social Security and minimum-
wage legislation, making these charters of labor of little
value to blacks.

The New Deal legislation on balance probably made
it harder, not easier, for blacks to enter the urban industrial economy. Their assets in the eyes of employers
had been their willingness, compelled by want and hunger, to accept below-standard wages and nonunion employment. The minimum-wage and pro-union legislation
denied or reduced the blacks' competitive advantage and
strengthened the unions' ability to exclude from employment those not already members. Similarly the housing
legislation and administrative practices of the New Deal
strengthened the barrier that protected the exclusiveness
of white neighborhoods and suburbs.

The New Deal restored and strengthened the American society and economy, but it was a racist society and
economy that were strengthened. The jobs, the homes,

167

the farms, the savings, the status of Americans were protected by federal action, but one of the things these possessions were protected against was the intrusion of blacks into "white" jobs and "white" neighborhoods. The New Deal did nothing to end segregation or to improve black education, or to open jobs to blacks, or to restore the vote to blacks.

In part this policy was due to the general restorative rather than the revolutionary goals of the New Deal; in part it was due to Roosevelt's dependence on Southern Congressional committee chairmen for the passage of essential legislation. But whatever the cause, the consequence was that the private practices that isolated blacks in low-paid unskilled employment in declining areas of the economy and in ghetto areas received tacit official sanction and reinforcement from the United States government.

And yet Roosevelt and the New Deal received the adoring support of most Negroes. The Northern urban Negro vote, which was to become far more crucial, shifted massively from the Republican to the Democratic party. There were two reasons for this. The New Deal aided the poor through work relief programs and welfare grants to which blacks were admitted. Though the administration of these programs tended to favor whites over blacks, poverty was so much worse among Negroes that any acts to ameliorate it were a special boon to the black community. Though blacks were still imprisoned in their low estate, the New Deal had softened its rigors.

More important was an emotional factor. President Roosevelt, and even more strikingly his wife, Eleanor, had a genuine compassion for the poor and disinherited generally, and both of them easily and naturally accepted Negroes as human beings and citizens. The quality of their concern flowed beyond the meager material gifts of the New Deal to bring hope and a feeling of recognition to blacks who had endured generations of numbing hostilities or indifferent contempt.

The Roosevelts' concern was part of a changing attitude that reached into the more sensitive elements of American society. The sufferings of the Depression had shattered complacency and awakened a sense of compassion. The racist ideas of Nazism had become odious and had forced Americans to examine their own consciences. This greater social concern was manifested in the critical and passionate tone of younger writers. Novelists like John Dos Passos and John Steinbeck and playwrights like Clifford Odets and Lillian Hellman, with dozens of less well-known writers of like views, savagely attacked the injustices of American society. Though the evils they exposed were those of poverty and economic oppression of blacks and whites alike, racial injustice itself was not ignored. More widespread attention was drawn to the remarkable generation of black writers who had emerged in the 1920s, and new voices of black anger like that of Richard Wright were widely heard.

Scholars too became newly critical of American life and turned to an examination of its social pathology, with special attention to poverty and racism. Especially notable was the work of the Institute for Research in Social Science at the University of North Carolina, where the work of Howard Odum, Rupert Vance, and their colleagues provided a solid factual basis for an understanding of Southern problems, including especially those of race. Other studies by economists, sociologists, anthropologists, and social psychologists began to accumulate the data that would underlie the remarkable series of Supreme Court decisions of the 1950s invalidating racist legislation. This new scholarly concern culminated in Gunnar Myrdal's massive study, *An American Dilemma*. With foundation support, Myrdal assembled in overwhelming and objective detail a picture of American racism that could not be ignored or evaded.

The economic and social liberalism of the 1930s and the more critical examination of American social patterns and traditions did not, however, lead to major changes in the actual role of blacks in the 1930s, with one important exception. More liberal labor leaders had become more and more actively dissatisfied with the conservative attitudes and the narrow goals of the traditional craft unions that dominated the American Federation of Labor and that spent much of their energies in protecting their narrow and specialized domains, often at the expense of other working men. The failure of these unions to play any important role in averting or mitigating the catastrophes of the Depression emphasized their growing irrelevance.

More liberal labor leaders believed that workers could have power only if organized in large unions by industry, cutting across craft lines. New unions, such as the United Automobile Workers, were formed; and older industrial unions, such as the United Mine Workers, joined with them in forming at first a Committee on Industrial Organization within the A. F. of L. and later a Congress of Industrial Organizations that seceded from it. These great industrial unions were inclusive, not exclusive. Their object was to embrace all the workers in an industry, not to preserve a specialized area of work for a limited membership. Hence they eagerly sought black members from the beginning. In major industries so organized—such as steel, rubber, automobile manufacture, and mining—most of which had employed blacks from World War I on, they now had union protection. This was of special significance in view of the increasingly rigid exclusivity of the craft unions as the Depression eliminated jobs.

No civil-rights legislation arose from the growing concern with racial justice that emerged in the 1930s, but it did affect the courts, which began to assume their later role as the voice of American conscience in racial matters. Prior to the late 1930s the federal courts had consistently construed the Constitution and relevant statutes in ways most prejudicial to the rights of blacks. Though later courts would not state so bluntly as Taney's in the Dred Scott case that Negroes had no rights white men were bound to respect, they came very close to this position. They had narrowed to meaninglessness the scope of federal civil-rights legislation. They had given official sanction to the practice of legal segregation under a transparently false concept of "separate but equal." While inventing ingenious rationalizations to extend the protection of the Fourteenth Amendment to corporations in ways not conceived when it was ratified, they denied the plain intentions of the same amendment when applied to Negroes. They solemnly held dozens of state laws constitutional, though clearly and admittedly intended to disfranchise blacks in open defiance of the Fifteenth Amendment, and found the grounds for doing so in the mere fact that race was not in explicit words made the criterion of voting. Private actions to discriminate in employment, in admission to places of entertainment and accommodation, and through restrictive covenants in the sale or leasing of real estate received the sanction and protection of the courts.

Indeed, almost the only Supreme Court decisions asserting the rights of blacks were handed down in cases involving statutes in which race was expressly made the criterion not merely for segregation but for a specific denial of rights. As early as 1917, in the case of *Buchanan* v. *Warley*, the Supreme Court had invalidated local legislation (as distinguished from private agreement) setting up zoning regulations explicitly requiring residential segregation on the basis of race.

In the 1930s, the Supreme Court began to express a broader concern for its role as a protector of individual rights generally. Its practice had been to sustain state legislation unless it was patently and unarguably unconstitutional and to assume that state legislators' assessment of facts and social conditions was accurate. The newer tendency of the Court was expressed in 1938 in a comment of Justice Harlan F. Stone in *U.S.* v. *Caroline Products* in which he said that the presumption of constitutionality should be narrower if it was a possible contravention of the Bill of Rights that was in question.

The Court had already begun to act in limited ways to put this tendency into effect. In decisions arising from the famous Scottsboro case, in which several Negro youths were tried for the alleged rape of two white girls, the Court in 1935 went beyond its earlier decisions that state law could not exclude blacks from juries to hold

that the systematic absence of blacks from jury panels
was in itself such evidence of exclusion as to entitle the
defendants to a new trial, even though there might have
been no overt official action to bar Negroes.

The Court also began to re-examine the realities of
the *Plessy* v. *Ferguson* doctrine of "separate but equal."
Having laid down the principle that separate accommodations were lawful so long as they were equal, the
Court had been willing to accept the findings of state
legislation and courts as to the fact of equality, which in
practice left blacks with no real protection against gross
discrimination. But in the case of *Missouri ex rel. Gaines*
v. *Canada,* the Court in 1938 held that for the state of
Missouri to refuse a black student admission to the University of Missouri Law School and instead to provide
his expenses in attending an out-of-state law school was
not giving him equal treatment and required his admission to the state school.

These were but the most tentative steps, but they were
to assume a great importance as the first evidence of the
Court's willingness to look beneath the surface of Southern statutes to the reality of Southern discriminatory
practices and to measure them against the Constitution.
Other decisions, though not involving racial matters, had
asserted the rights of minorities and dissidents to express
their views without being stifled or punished by local
ordinances or state laws—decisions that later were to be
invaluable to organizations determined to assert black
rights in the face of Southern hostility.

By 1940 Justice Hugo Black could truly say, in *Cham-
bers* v. *Florida,* that "No higher duty, no more solemn
responsibility, rests upon this Court, than that of translat-

ing into living law and maintaining this constitutional shield deliberately planned and inscribed for the benefit of every human being subject to our Constitution—of whatever race, creed or persuasion."

CHAPTER TEN

In Which War Renews the Uses of Blacks

THE LONG DEPRESSION that had been only mitigated by the effects of the New Deal began to yield in 1940 to the economic drives of war. British and for a time French purchases of supplies and the growing demands of the American rearmament effort awoke the economy and opened hundreds of thousands and then millions of jobs. The enactment of the draft law and the building up of the American armed forces in 1940 and 1941 required other millions of men. There was a demand again for men, all men, blacks included. Throughout the late nineteenth and the twentieth centuries, the black community, in addition to supplying agricultural labor and personal service, had served as a labor reserve to be called in for strike-breaking, for unpleasant or ill-paid labor for which other workmen could not be found, and for times of special need—a reserve that could be dismissed or discarded when the need was past. Now, in 1940 and 1941, as in 1917 the nation needed this black reserve to fill out the ranks of the armed services and build up the labor force.

But this time there was a difference. In 1917 blacks entered both the armed services and the civilian labor force at the bottom and remained at the lowest levels. In the earlier war there were no black Marines and no black members of the Navy except for messmen. Black soldiers were grouped in segregated regiments and labor battalions, usually assigned to menial and noncombatant duties and served under white officers. Few black civilian workers in World War I were able to get the highly paid new jobs in war industries; instead they filled the places of stockyard and railroad laborers who had themselves moved on to better work.

These patterns were repeated in the early months of mobilization for World War II. Blacks moved again from the draft board into the labor battalion and stood excluded at the gates of the unionized war plants. But it was a more knowing generation, more conscious of rights, more organized to assert them. And in 1941 there were many whites, prodded in their consciences by Nazi racism and inspired by the humane emotions of the New Deal, who were prepared to support their cause, as there had not been in 1917. Negro protests were vigorous from the beginning but were smothered with soft inattention by President Roosevelt. Just as the President had habitually put aside racial problems in order not to disturb his smooth relations with Southern Congressional committee chairmen, he was ready now to put them aside in order not to add problems either to the mobilization of the armed forces or to the organization of war production.

A Committee on the Participation of Negroes in the National Defense Program had been formed in 1940, but it was unable to gain meaningful concessions. Public statements by the President in general opposition to segregation went unheeded in practice, as did vague anti-discrimination language in the Draft Act. Not until shortly before the election of 1940 was President Roosevelt willing even to see a delegation of Negro leaders, and on that occasion they received a total rebuff. Representatives of the NAACP, the Urban League, and the Sleeping Car Porters asked for integration of the armed services and the removal of all racial barriers within them; but the War Department, with the President's approval, simply reiterated its intention of keeping blacks segregated in all-black regiments.

In these circumstances, A. Philip Randolph, who had been one of the rebuffed spokesmen in the meeting with the President, decided on a mass public appeal against racial injustice on the war effort. He envisioned this as taking the form of a march on Washington in which 10,000 blacks—a figure later raised to 100,000—would come to the capital to lay before the President and Congress their demands for equal treatment in the armed forces and in war industry. As the plans matured and the march began to take the shape of imminent reality, the President and his advisers became disturbed. It was increasingly evident that to ignore or deny black demands would be more disruptive of the war effort than to concede them. When various public statements about equality and nondiscrimination failed to impress the sponsors of the march, the President, on June 25, 1941, a week before the march was to begin, signed a long-sought Executive Order (the famous E. O. 8802) forbidding racial discrimination by defense contractors and by agencies of the federal government and establishing a Committee on Fair Employment Practice to oversee its execution. In spite of the fact that nothing had been gained in the fight against discrimination in the armed services, the march was called off—officially it was "postponed"—and the Negro community awaited the result of the Executive Order.

The results were important if by no means complete. Major defense contractors, most of whom had never used blacks in other than menial jobs, at least cracked open their doors to skilled Negro workmen. And some opened them wide, offering training programs to build up the factory skills of employees whose experience had been confined to farming, personal service, or common labor. The aircraft industry, previously completely closed to Negroes except for janitorial jobs, had hired more than 100,000 by war's end; and other defense industries had made notable, if less striking, progress. Hundreds of thousands of blacks had received training in government-financed programs that would prepare them for peacetime jobs as well. And other hundreds of thousands had been employed by the government itself. And for the first time a substantial proportion of these were hired in clerical, secretarial, administrative, and professional positions.

The Fair Employment Practices program, however, was bitterly opposed by Congressional leaders from the South and never really commanded the special attention or vigorous support of the President. The FEPC itself was shifted about in the government, housed in hostile agencies, and denied adequate funds and authority. For all the notable progress in certain plants and industries, a heavy burden of discrimination still lay on blacks at the war's end, especially in the quality of employment. Even in industries that hired blacks without restriction, few indeed became foremen or supervisors or were raised to more highly skilled jobs. Union construction jobs remained almost entirely closed to blacks with a few exceptions, such as hod carriers. Also closed were jobs involving dealings with the white public as salesmen, receptionists, insurance agents, intercity bus drivers, and the like.

For hundreds of thousands of blacks who were helped to better jobs, even the limited practical achievements of FEPC in the war years were of course very important. But the principal importance of Executive Order 8802 was probably as a precedent for future policy. For the first time the equal treatment of blacks in employment had been defined as a national policy and a matter of appropriate governmental concern. Prior to 1940 almost no white, whatever his feelings of the injustice of employment policies that closed opportunities to blacks, would have thought it legal or proper for the federal government to tell a private employer, even one with a federal contract, whom he might or might not hire. Nor did most whites see anything unusual or improper about the closing of whole categories of jobs to Negroes. Indeed, the categorization of some jobs as "white" and others as "black" had been taken for granted as a normal and appropriate practice. For the first time, such segregation and discrimination in private employment—even if only private employment in the fulfillment of government contracts—was defined as a wrong, and as a wrong remediable by government action.

In the 1930s the federal government itself had become almost completely segregated in employment. Except for token jobs, blacks had been hired only as laborers, messengers, drivers, janitors, and similar occupations that were considered "black" jobs in private employment. Laws and Civil Service regulations in general neither required nor forbade discrimination. Civil Service applications included photographs of the applicants, and agencies were free to choose whomever they would from the top three applicants on the register. This latitude allowed an almost complete barring of blacks from even those professional, administrative, and higher clerical positions that were under the Civil Service merit system. The elimination of photographs and other indications of race from applications, increasingly searching Civil Service Commission and FEPC checks on the employment and promotion policies of agencies, and queries as to the number of employees of minority groups in various grades did much to lessen the rigidity of discrimination. It became possible for blacks to hope for initial appointment to secretarial, clerical, and administrative jobs, though their subsequent assignments and promotion remained weighted with prejudice. And a black could not expect any really responsible federal job unless as a symbol or in a position especially concerned with racial problems or relations. But again, the public doctrine had been firmly established, however imperfectly applied, that blacks must have equal treatment in federal employment.

The elimination of discrimination in the armed services had been one of the objectives of the groups organizing the March on Washington, but it was not included in the settlement that averted the demonstration. Military segregation survived the war, and at the war's end as well as at its beginning blacks were enrolled in separate units in all services. Some steps, however, were taken to reduce discrimination. For the first time blacks were admitted to the Marine Corps and to general service in the Navy. Black combat regiments were put into service, as well as black-manned naval vessels and Air Corps squadrons. The training of black officers in all services was stepped up. In the armed forces, as in federal and federally related private employment, an untenable compromise position had been reached. The theoretical and legal justifications for discrimination had been destroyed and could never be successfully reasserted; but the implications of this policy conclusion had been only very partially achieved. The country could not relapse to the early twentieth-century position in which discrimination was legally and morally acceptable, nor could it achieve in actual life the integrated and equalitarian society its new assumptions called for. The tension between the theoretical and the actual in race relations would remain as a torturing and unresolvable problem in American life for decades to come: the discrimination that remained but could not be justified or even rationalized, and the equality that was proclaimed but could not be achieved.

The war's end transferred these conflicts from the area of temporary wartime policy to that of permanent peacetime application. Would the armed forces return to their former peacetime discrimination or take advantage of the relaxation of pressure to work out a genuine integration? Would the federal government continue its efforts to assure equality of employment opportunity now that it did not need to try to win black support for the war?

Beyond these specifics, would the idealism that sustained the war effort and that had been rooted in the New Deal itself survive to create in American society the freedom from racial discrimination to which it was pledged?

The idealism remained strong, stronger and longer-lasting than after our other major wars, but it faced strong counterforces. Among them was a revulsion against the war itself and all the sacrifices it entailed and against the administration that had required them. In the first postwar election, in 1946, the Republican party carried both Senate and House in a mood of "return to normalcy." Though President Harry Truman, who had succeeded upon President Roosevelt's death in April 1945, was more forthright than Roosevelt on racial issues, there was little he could achieve in the face of the conservative control of Congress.

In January 1947 Truman appointed a Committee on Civil Rights charged with making a sweeping survey of the measures required to achieve a racially equal society in the United States. The committee's report was submitted in October 1947 and recommended effective federal legislation in almost every aspect of civil rights. It proposed, among other measures, strengthening existing laws and enacting new statutes on lynching, voting rights, and discrimination in employment. The creation of several new bodies to oversee enforcement of these measures was recommended: a Civil Rights Commission, a Civil Rights Division in the Department of Justice, a corresponding Congressional committee, and a permanent Fair Employment Practices Commission. President Truman put himself fully behind the recommendations of the committee and in February 1948 submitted them to Congress with proposals for legislation to carry them into effect.

In doing so—given the make-up of Congress—Truman was establishing a position for the campaign rather than seriously expecting legislation. His support of civil rights, backed by the Democratic national convention, led to a secession of Southern opponents, who backed Strom Thurmond of South Carolina as a states' rights candidate for President, and it did not prevent a further secession on the left, which led to the creation of a Progressive Party supporting Henry Wallace. Nevertheless, Truman was surprisingly elected over these opponents and over a too confident Republican candidate, Thomas E. Dewey. And an essential part of his margin of victory was the Negro votes which he had so fully earned.

The foreign crises of Truman's second administration allowed him to give only limited attention to domestic racial issues, and no cooperation could be won from Congress. Neverthless, Truman did what he could. A Federal Contracts Committee was created to carry on as much of the work of the FEPC as was possible without legislation. Steady pressure was exercised toward the elimination of discrimination in hiring and promotion within the executive branch of the federal government itself. Following a Supreme Court decision refusing to permit the courts to be used to enforce racially restrictive covenants, federal housing agencies ceased to encourage such covenants as a protection of the mortgageable value of houses.

The foreign crisis itself produced one advance. President Truman had ordered the end of all racial segregation and assignments on the basis of race in the armed services. To put this order into general practice and to change the generations-old structures of the services might have taken many years in peacetime. But a new army had to be created for the Korean conflict, and it was an integrated Army, the first in American history. Though covert racial discrimination in promotions may well have continued to exist, by the end of the Korean war the Army was probably the most fully integrated institution in American life.

By 1953, when President Truman left the White House, the legal structure of race relations was almost unchanged. But a standard had been erected. The conviction that blacks were indeed American citizens, whose relation to their government must not be affected by their skin color, and that the United States should be, even though it was not, dedicated to the proposition that all men are created equal had been clearly stated by the President—and for the first time in all the country's history. It was the kind of statement which, once made, could never thereafter be easily escaped.

•

CHAPTER ELEVEN

In Which the Legal Position of Blacks Is Revolutionized

In the early years of the Eisenhower administration the United States had its first opportunity since the 1920s to dispose of an economic surplus. There had been the Depression and then the war. The Truman years had been full of emergencies: the atomic bomb, war's end, the creation of the United Nations, the cold war, the Berlin blockade and airlift, the Marshall Plan, the Point Four program, and finally the Korean war. With the close of that agony, the American people could again make choices about their future freed from the demands of emergencies. These included choices about the future of blacks in American society. One set of the decisions they made related to the legal status of blacks and was embodied in a series of Supreme Court decisions and legislative acts. Another set related to the kind of economy we would have and the uses to which our resources would be put. In many ways these two sets of emerging decisions conflicted, and the tensions of American life over the following decades largely arose from that conflict.

The decisions relating to the legal status of blacks were the clearest and easiest to follow. The basic question in law, on which all else depended, was especially simple. It was whether the Constitution permitted blacks to be considered as a separate class of persons who could be treated differently from whites in the laws and by the administrative actions of government. If such separate treatment were permissible, then it would be difficult to hold *any* discriminatory legislation unconstitutional. If one may constitutionally treat blacks and whites differently under the law, to what degree and what manner becomes a matter for legislative discretion rather than constitutional right. As we have seen, even a guarantee of equal though separate treatment dissolves in the fluid concepts of equality. But if blacks are entitled to identical treatment with whites under the law, it would be equally impossible to *uphold* any discriminatory law. For years before 1954 the courts had nibbled at discrimination, invalidating some laws and upholding others. But logic now demanded either a relegation of blacks to a constitutionally second-class position or a blanket invalidation of laws that treated them differently from whites.

For decades the courts had evaded this confrontation by formally accepting three myths: that laws segregating blacks and whites, as in schools or on trains, might result in their equal, even though separate, treatment and hence not injure blacks; that laws that did not mention race but merely abridged the rights of the poor or uneducated, such as the requirement of literacy tests or poll taxes to vote, did not discriminate against blacks; and that private actions taken systematically to treat blacks unequally in the exercise of property rights or other rights guaranteed by the state were only private matters which the authority of government could not reach. By pretending to believe as judges what they knew as men to be false, the courts had been able to uphold as "separate and equal" segregated school systems in which the per-student expenditure was ten or twelve times as high for white students as for black. They had been able to approve as not in violation of the Fifteenth Amendment literacy tests which, as administered, almost totally eliminated black voting within a state. And they had upheld actions of a political party to bar blacks from voting in primary elections or of a group of private landholders to covenant among themselves not to sell to blacks as though these were not actions stamped with a public character.

But these subterfuges proved increasingly uncomfortable, and ultimately intolerable, to judicial consciences sensitized by the struggle against Nazism and by the quiet but implacable pressure of the NAACP and other black organizations. By 1954 the Supreme Court had moved, step by slow step, toward the abandonment of these myths and the recognition of the legal consequences of an acceptance of genuine black equality and indeed identity with other citizens.

The Supreme Court had already held, before 1954, that if public accommodations in interstate commerce were to be separate they must be truly and wholly equal and subsequently, and significantly, that for a state to require segregation at all in a portion of an interstate bus trip was unconstitutional (though as a burden on interstate commerce rather than as a denial of rights of the passenger). It had declared restrictive covenants forbidding the sale of houses to blacks to be unenforceable in the courts. It had denied the right of states to bar blacks from professional schools unless truly equal professional education was offered blacks within the state, or to segregate blacks within such a school. It had invalidated trials of Negroes before juries drawn from panels from which Negroes were excluded. It had held unconstitutional the more blatant subterfuges by which blacks were denied the vote through the pretense that political parties were private clubs, or through literacy tests administered with cynical and open intent to disfranchise blacks. In these decisions the Court had not yet brought itself to deny the constitutionality of the separate legal treatment of blacks in itself; but it had given a more nearly real meaning to the concept of equality in the doctrine of "separate and equal." And it had shown a willingness to look behind the public letter of the law and examine the actuality of the law's application to the daily circumstances of life. By the 1950s the Court had been made ready to confront the central core of the legal and constitutional problem of black status in America.

The opportunity to do so came in a series of cases decided by the Court in 1954 which dealt with the segregation of the races in the public schools. In these cases the plaintiffs attacked not the inferiority of the separate black schools but their separateness. To distinguish blacks from whites in the application of the law was inherently discriminatory, they pleaded, even if in buildings, equipment, materials, and teacher salary and competence the schools were entirely equal. And the Supreme Court agreed, not narrowly but unanimously, in a culmination of the long drive toward equality and beyond that toward the erasure of racial criteria from American law (*Brown* v. *Board of Education*).

The opinion was a brief one. Its essence was expressed in a few words: "We come then to the question presented: Does segregation of children in public schools solely on the basis of race, even though the physical facilities and other 'tangible' factors may be equal, deprive the children of the minority group of equal educational opportunities? We believe that it does. . . . We conclude that in the field of public education 'separate but equal' has no place. Separate educational facilities are inherently unequal."

This decision represented a final resolution of our constitutional ambiguities about race, the final acceptance of Justice Harlan's dissenting view in the *Plessy* v. *Ferguson* decision of 1896: "Our constitution is color-blind and neither knows nor tolerates classes among citizens." The many appellate-court decisions that followed the Brown decision simply extended this conclusion to other fields. Explicit state action to bar blacks from living in "white" areas had already been invalidated. The other areas in which the laws of many states explicitly required the segregation or differential treatment of blacks included public transportation, places of public assembly or accommodation, and marriage.

Even prior to 1954 the Supreme Court had so closely approached the banning of segregation in interstate travel that the Interstate Commerce Commission in 1955 followed its lead and, without awaiting suits, barred segregation in interstate rail and bus travel by administrative regulation. The following year the Court, in *Gayle* v. *Browder,* extended this ban to intrastate travel as well. A series of decisions from 1960 to 1962 forbade segregation in privately managed restaurants operated in bus terminals, airports, and municipal parking areas (*Boynton* v. *Virginia; Burton* v. *Wilmington Parking Authority; Turner* v. *Memphis*).

Laws denying persons of differing races the right to marry came more slowly before the courts since there were fewer likely plaintiffs. But after nibbling at the problem in earlier decisions, the Supreme Court, in *Loving* v. *Virginia,* carried through the logic of its earlier decisions and ruled racial limitations on marriage unconstitutional.

Meanwhile it had been demonstrated once more that the handing down of a Supreme Court decision does not in itself change social reality. The application of the Brown decision holding racial segregation in the public schools unconstitutional had been resisted not only by illegal force but by a variety of legal devices throughout the South. A great deal of additional litigation was necessary to clarify and enforce it. These cases arose with painful slowness because they depended on the initiative, courage, and resources of individual plaintiffs. In a second hearing of the Brown case in 1955, in which the Supreme Court reviewed the decrees of the lower courts effectuating its earlier holding, the Court stated that existing segregation must be ended "with all deliberate speed," a phrase seized on by Southern officials as justifying action of glacial gradualism even in those cases in which suits by local plaintiffs forced any change at all. In 1958, in *Cooper* v. *Aaron,* and again in 1964, in *Griffin* v. *County School Board,* the Court was compelled to push for faster implementation and finally to require the immediate termination of all remaining segregation resulting from the prior operation of dual school systems.

Meanwhile it had to confront a variety of devices which sought to perpetuate segregation in practice without overtly violating the letter of the Brown decision. "Freedom of choice" schemes that made explicit reference to race were held illegal in 1963 in *Goss* v. *Board of Education,* and finally the Court ruled conclusively against any form of dual school system, even when complete freedom was granted students to choose the school they would attend. The extreme white reaction to the Court's rulings was to close public schools entirely rather than have them be integrated. In some cases the school tax funds were made available for scholarships to permit students to attend private schools. Varying forms of these practices were outlawed as carried out in St. Helena Parish, Louisiana, and Prince Edward County, Virginia, in 1962 and 1964.

As a result of this series of cases, the Supreme Court in the decade following the Brown decision had made it abundantly clear that any action by federal, state, or local authority that discriminated in any way whatever among citizens on the basis of their race or color was unconstitutional. But these decisions did very little to end or even to reduce the actual discrimination that blacks encountered. For generations the Southern states had maintained an almost complete exclusion of blacks from the polls, in the face of the explicit and incontrovertible provisions of the Fifteenth Amendment forbidding any abridgment of the right to vote because of race, color, or previous condition of servitude. They had done so by an array of legal devices that discrimi-

nated against the poorer and less educated and that were
further twisted in their covert application doubly to
penalize the ignorance and poverty of blacks while
largely ignoring those of whites. A similar ingenuity
erected a maze of legal devices to sustain segregation,
which had to be overcome slowly and obstacle by obstacle through individual actions.

The judicial decisions themselves did nothing to bring
into play the enormous powers of the executive branch
of the government save as it might be called on to enforce
a specific order of a court. During the decade following
the Brown decision, and especially during the remaining
seven years of the Eisenhower administration, the federal
executive stood aloof from civil-rights litigation, view-
ing it as though a controversy among private parties in
which its intervention, except when necessary to execute
the orders of the Court, was uncalled for and even improper. This meant that the whole burden of enforcing
the Constitution of the United States against the massed
public authority of state and local governments in the
South determined to flout it was left to individual plaintiffs with limited means and with few lawyers willing to
take their cases, plaintiffs who, moreover, must act in
the face of threats of being fired from jobs, driven from
farms, denied credit, and even of being beaten or killed.
In the circumstances it is remarkable that as many cases
reached the courts as did, but even in the aggregate they
touched the great mass of segregation at only a few tiny
points.

Behind the opposition of Southern public officials
stood the organized determination of dominant white
groups in the South to maintain the segregation and sub-

ordination of blacks. That determination was expressed in concerted private actions as well as public. The doors of schools here and there might be opened to all races by a specific court order issued pursuant to the Brown decision, but threats, bullying, and ostracism awaited the black child who walked through them. Local officials might admit that they had no authority to deny a black citizen the vote because of his race, but private menace as well as the official frustration of unfair literacy tests and capriciously closed registration offices stood ominously in his way.

Most important and most discouraging of all, though the courts might strike down laws and ordinances *requiring* the segregation of the races in hotels, restaurants, lunch counters, auditoriums, swimming pools and the like, the private owners of such facilities remained free to bar whom they would. And they obeyed the community mores as faithfully as they had obeyed the Jim Crow laws. The Supreme Court of the United States of America had said that a black man was a man like any other man, but the theater ticket-taker in a Southern town was still free to turn him away, the motel clerk along the highway to send him on weary in the night, the lunch-counter waitress to have him thrown out hungering, even the filling-station proprietor to lock the restrooms against him. Though the courts would not force a white property owner to *refuse* to sell or rent to a black in obedience to a restrictive covenant, neither did they assert the power to compel him to *accept* a black tenant or buyer. It was only public bodies and instruments of interstate commerce that were compelled to deal evenhandedly with men of all races. And under the decision of the Supreme Court in the civil-rights cases of 1883, this was as far as the Fourteenth Amendment extended the powers of the Congress.

For more than eighty years, since the passage of the Civil Rights Act of 1875, the use or threat of filibusters by Southern Senators had prevented the exercise even of those powers of Congress that were unquestionable under the Thirteenth, Fourteenth, and Fifteenth Amendments. So flagrant, however, was the lawlessness of Southern refusal to obey the Supreme Court's decisions or to comply with the Fifteenth Amendment, so visible had this lawlessness become in the days of television, and so effective had become the organization of a national opposition to racial discrimination that it again became possible for Congress to legislate on the issue. Between 1957 and 1968 no fewer than five major civil-rights acts were passed. These had two goals. One was to overcome official subterfuges used to evade compliance with existing constitutional requirements for equal voting opportunity and for the elimination of racial segregation in schools and other public facilities. The other was to establish new laws forbidding private discrimination in public accommodations, housing, and employment.

The first of these were enacted in 1957 after the Senate had succeeded, for the first time in three-quarters of a century, in breaking a Southern filibuster against civil-rights legislation. But the cost of breaking the filibuster was the acceptance of amendments that so emasculated the bill as to make it nearly meaningless. Many of its original supporters voted for its final form only reluctantly, and Senator Richard Russell of Georgia, who had led the opposition, exulted in its transformation as the "sweetest victory" in his twenty-five years in Congress. The principal thrust of the bill as it had passed the House of Representatives had been contained in a section empowering the Attorney General to bring suit to enjoin those acting to deny or withhold the constitutional rights of citizens. This would have struck directly at the principal defense of Southern opponents of civil rights. This defense was simply to ignore Supreme Court decisions until action in a particular locality was compelled by the suit of an individual plaintiff. The opponents were able to rely on the lack of lawyers and resources and the carefully engendered fears of potential plaintiffs to assure that there would be so few local suits as not to require any serious enforcement of or respect for the Supreme Court's actions. If the enormous power of the Justice Department were applied to the enforcement of the Constitution, this whole defense might collapse.

This key section of the bill was abandoned as part of the price of gaining the two-thirds majority required to close the debate. What was left was the creation of a temporary Civil Rights Commission with no authority save to investigate and report; authorization to the President to appoint an Assistant Attorney General to head a new Civil Rights Division in the Justice Department; and a provision making interference with the right to register and vote illegal, whether or not committed under color of law, and entitling those injured to injunctive relief. The Attorney General was authorized to seek such an injunction and to do so in anticipation of, as well as in the face of, such interference; but he had this power only with respect to the particular voting provisions. One other price of passage of the bill was to deny a federal judge the right to impose a fine of more than $300 or a sentence of more than forty-five days in punishment for criminal contempt of court without a jury trial unless the contempt were committed in the court's presence.

In its direct effect the 1957 act proved almost completely without meaning. The difficulties of action by the Attorney General were so great that only one trivial intervention by his office took place over the next two years. The disfranchisement of Negroes continued undisturbed, and the act did not even attempt to reach other black grievances. But two of its most innocuous provisions were to yield indirect results. The very frustration created in the new Civil Rights Division by its impotence stimulated it to urge and to draft new legislation, and the vigorous Civil Rights Commission appointed under the chairmanship of John Hannah issued hard-hitting reports that supplied the factual bases for the new proposals.

The result was a renewed attack on civil-rights problems in the next Congress, culminating in the passage of the Civil Rights Act of 1960. Most of its provisions were narrowly aimed at specific means of Southern resistance that had outraged most Americans. Obstruction of any order of a federal court was made a crime. A favorite means of evading legal action against discrimination in applying the voting laws was forbidden by a provision that all election records must be retained for twenty-two months and made available for inspection. Bombings had become a horrible means of intimidating blacks and their white supporters, and one provision of the new law made it a federal crime to transport explosives across state lines with intent to use them unlawfully or to flee to another state to avoid arrest or prosecution for bombing. The primary purpose of this was to bring the FBI into the investigation of such incidents. Efforts were made to include a system of federal registrars who could register black voters directly, bypassing all resistance by local officials; but this was watered down to provide for voting referees instead. These could be appointed by a federal district court upon application by the Attorney General and a finding that a pattern of discrimination existed. Referees could hear applications from those wishing to be registered but prevented by local discrimination. Upon finding that the applicants were qualified under state law, the referees could certify their names to the court, which, after notice to state officials and an opportunity for hearing, could order the applicants' registration. This procedure was to prove too complex to be useful in practice.

The 1960 act, like its predecessor of 1957, accomplished little. It dealt with peripheral matters and removed some of the obstacles to proceedings by the Attorney General in voting-rights cases. But those proceedings themselves, pressing individual cases now here, now there, wearily through the courts, were powerless to affect in any fundamental way the regionwide determination to prevent black voting. The Attorney General was given no power to sue to enforce other rights of blacks, and private discrimination remained beyond the reach of any law.

And so the statute law remained, well meaning and impotent, until the public was finally aroused by the events of 1963. Brutal and unpunished murders of blacks and of white civil-rights workers by vigilantes and Southern public officials, savage repression in Birmingham, Selma, and other cities, and finally the assassination of President Kennedy combined to produce a profound revulsion of opinion. And it brought into the Presidency the overflowing energy and superb legislative skills of Lyndon Johnson, now fully dedicated to the enforcement of civil rights. This combination of drives was finally able to overcome the most determined of all filibusters and to enact at last, in 1964 and 1965, two civil-rights acts with teeth. The 1964 act, though it dealt further with specific barriers to voting, was primarily concerned with segregation. The 1965 act dealt comprehensively and radically with voting restraints.

In 1964 Congress made it a federal crime to apply a literacy or other voting test in a racially discriminatory way, even though the test itself might make no mention of race or color. Literacy tests were required to be in writing and to be preserved so that discrimination in their use could be discovered and proved. Voting-rights cases could have prompt hearings in a special federal court to prevent the delays that had made so many earlier actions fruitless.

But the 1964 act went far beyond voting. It attacked three other major areas of discrimination directly and vigorously. For the first time since 1875, Congress made unlawful any private discrimination against blacks in places of public accommodation affecting or affected by interstate commerce. These included hotels, restaurants, theaters, sports arenas or stadiums, and gasoline stations. The Attorney General was given authority to intervene in cases of discrimination in such places as well as in publicly owned or operated facilities. For the first time the power and majesty of the United States government could intervene directly and comprehensively to assure recognition of the constitutional rights of its citizens without leaving it to the chance of scattered individual suits by poor and vulnerable plaintiffs. These were provisions that had been sought in vain in the Civil Rights Acts of 1957 and 1960.

Moreover, the 1964 act provided Washington with its strongest weapon of all: a mandate against the grant of federal funds to any state or local activity practicing racial segregation or discrimination. Since local schools and hospitals, especially in the South, were heavily dependent on federal aid, this one provision was more effective than any other in forcing at least an ostensible, and often an actual, end of the discriminatory administration of such institutions.

The remaining major provision outlawed both racial and sexual discrimination in employment in businesses engaged in interstate commerce, which was very broadly defined. It applied initially only to those businesses with a labor force of more than one hundred, but it was to be extended gradually to employers of twenty-five or more. Labor unions as well as employers were made subject to its provisions. The terms were sweeping but the enforcement provisions were mild, relying heavily on conciliation, negotiation, and the use of state legislation and agencies.

The Attorney General was at last given the authority to initiate or intervene in suits to enforce school desegregation as well as for the protection of other civil rights. The Commissioner of Education was instructed to make a study of racial segregation at all educational levels

throughout the United States and to give technical assistance to schools in the process of desegregation. Funds
were authorized to give training to educators in methods
to accomplish integration smoothly. Ten full years after
the Brown decision of 1954 the federal government was
for the first time arming itself to enforce the constitutional mandate set forth in that decision. Throughout
that decade it had been content to do no more than enforce the occasional judicial injunction requiring desegregation that resulted from the scattered suits of individual parents, and even that often with apparent reluctance.
As a result, save in such border states as had themselves
enforced the decision in good faith, school desegregation
had made only infinitesimal progress by 1964. But now at
last the government was firmly addressing itself to the
problem and was provided with the legal weapons that
would enable it to do so comprehensively. As we shall
see, even this formidable set of provisions did not assure
actual integration in the classroom, but it did mean the
early end of dual school systems segregated on specifically racial grounds.

Other and less significant provisions strengthened the
hands of the Civil Rights Commission, required the
Bureau of the Census under the guidance of the commission to make a survey of registration and voting
statistics, and empowered federal courts to regain control
as necessary of civil-rights cases remanded to state courts.

Voting, which had been the primary subject of attention in the ineffective acts of 1957 and 1960, was not
dealt with in the 1964 act except in the call for the survey
and report noted above. But the damning evidence of the
continued exclusion of blacks from the polls yielded by

that survey jolted Congress into still another act in 1965, this time devoted entirely to voting. And the data from the survey provided the basis for a new method of assaulting black disfranchisement. The Voting Rights Act of 1965 defined the areas in which unlawful restrictions on voting could be presumed as those which employed literacy tests or similar devices and in which fewer than half of those of voting age had voted in the 1964 Presidential election. This was found to include Alabama, Georgia, Louisiana, Mississippi, South Carolina, Virginia, and twenty-six eastern North Carolina counties. In addition, an occasional scattered county elsewhere was included, generally by statistical accident.

In the jurisdictions so defined, all literacy tests and similar devices were forbidden, and federal registrars could be appointed to register all those who sought to vote. No new test or device could be adopted in those areas unless submitted to and approved by the Attorney General. Even in areas not so defined, the Justice Department was given full authority to intervene in or to initiate actions to assure the voting rights of blacks. Puerto Ricans were further aided by a provision that any one who had completed the sixth grade of a school under American jurisdiction should be presumed to be literate, whatever the language of instruction. For the first time, any black who wanted to register and vote now had a realistic opportunity to do so. Because voting was totally under public control, and because the system of federal registrars was under centralized national direction, it was possible to enforce the antidiscrimination provisions of this act far more completely than earlier provisions relating to housing, employment, and public accommodations.

In one major area yet another law was needed to complete the panoply of statutory and judicial guarantees. That was housing. It had become apparent that the most festering of all problems affecting blacks lay in the central ghettos of Northern cities. Expensive, overcrowded, squalid, and deteriorating housing bred crime and social disorder and bitterness. Residential segregation defeated efforts at the integration of schools and impeded programs to give equal employment opportunities to blacks, especially in the rapidly growing suburban plants and in service and white-collar jobs. In the long run perhaps an even more destructive consequence of the new ghettos was to separate the life patterns of blacks and whites. For all the equal-rights laws on the books of Northern states, whites and blacks in Northern cities lived with far less human contact with one another than in the rural areas and small towns of the South. It was the segregation in ghettos more than anything else that led the Kerner Commission (the President's Commission to Investigate the Cause of Social Disorders) to report in 1967 that the United States was becoming two nations, one black and one white.

The last of the series of civil-rights acts passed during the fifteen years following the Brown decision was that of 1968, addressed primarily to the housing problem. Certain extraneous provisions were added to the bill as it progressed through Congress, including extensive legislation relating to the civil rights of American Indians. Southern resentment led also to the inclusion of sections increasing the powers of the federal government to deal with riots and disorder. It was made a federal offense to injure, intimidate, or interfere with anyone in the exercise of his civil rights. But the principal thrust of the act was to lessen discrimination and segregation in housing. It was made a federal crime to discriminate against anyone because of race, color, or national origin in the sale or rental of housing. The only exceptions were in connection with the sale or rental of individually owned single-family houses without the use of a real-estate agent and the rental of a room or apartment in what is essentially a private home. Rather elaborate enforcement procedures were set forth, relying heavily on state and local agencies and on voluntary cooperation. Had effective enforcement been achieved, this act would have gone far to end the compulsory ghetto and free the Negro to seek housing wherever he wished and his means would permit.

The series of judicial decisions and federal statutes, many of them paralleled by state legislation, constituted a major legal revolution. Prior to 1954, in the states in which most blacks lived the laws not only permitted but required their segregation in schools, on public transportation, and in places of public accommodation. Whatever the pretenses to comply with the "separate and equal" provisions of the Plessy decision, the separate arrangements made for Negroes were in fact vastly inferior. Black schools received a fraction of the support of those for whites, the "back of the bus" symbolized the transportation facilities, and a Southern Negro, no matter how wealthy, well dressed, and well behaved, might spend his life without ever entering a good hotel, eating at a good restaurant, attending a professional concert or a legitimate theater, visiting a white church, swimming in a municipal pool, playing tennis on a municipal court, or bathing at a public beach.

And while the states, with the acquiescence of the federal courts, required segregation in all these aspects of life, they expected and supported parallel action by private individuals and groups to maintain segregation in the areas not reached by the state directly. Private employers and labor unions barred blacks from all but the meanest jobs; white owners and brokers of real property barred them from all but the meanest houses; white custom barred them from the churches and social circles of whites. All of these acts of private discrimination expressed the sense of the Southern communities and had the police on call to support them.

Within fifteen years the legal support of segregation and discrimination had been withdrawn. Every statute requiring such prejudicial treatment had been repealed or held unconstitutional directly or by implication, every judicial decision supporting segregation reversed or overruled, administrative actions to discriminate enjoined. But not only had legally required differentiation of the races been outlawed. The law moved into those areas of private action once thought to be beyond its reach and explicitly denied the right of private individuals to discriminate in housing, in employment, and in public accommodation. From the enforcer of segregation the law was transformed in one short epoch to its foe. By 1968 the black was guaranteed, in statute books and court decisions, his full equality with all Americans in every action by which government touched his life. And the forces of government were required to help him assert that same equality in employment and housing and trains and buses and restaurants and theaters. Public policy, in its formal expression, had diametrically reversed itself.

But society is a vast organism whose actions are by no means all determined by its central legal system. While the revolution in law was taking place, enormous social and economic changes were going on as well. These changes were to transform the roles whites needed blacks to play in American life, and for most blacks were to alter their lives more dramatically than acts of Court and Congress.

CHAPTER TWELVE

In Which a New Affluence Further Impoverishes Poor Blacks

WHILE THE SUPREME COURT and the Congress arrived at the series of decisions that revolutionized the legal status of blacks, the government and people of the United States were making another set of decisions about the shape of the American economy and society— decisions that further exiled the majority of blacks from fruitful participation in the national life.

The close of the Korean war ended a generation of self-denial for the American people. The Depression, World War II, the immediate crises of the postwar years, and the Korean conflict itself had barred them from the golden time they looked for. Peace in Asia and the relaxation of relations with Russia that followed the death of Stalin brought a long-deferred opportunity to devote resources to needs at home. For the first time since the 1920s there was a real chance to choose the ways in which American life would use newly opened riches.

The basic decisions were made in an unplanned coincidence of government and private actions. There were five major ways in which the Americans spent their newly freed resources:

1. In a rapid application of scientific and technological advances to increasing productivity.

2. In providing new housing to overcome the deficit arising from a generation of restraints on construction and from the explosive creation of new families in the postwar years.

3. In providing a new generation of electric household appliances to the majority of American homes: television, air-conditioning, dishwashers, freezers, washing and drying machines, and dozens of others.

4. In making automobiles generally available to almost all Americans and providing the highways and services that made it possible to reorganize society around new patterns of mobility.

5. In creating an extensive jet air-transport system replacing railroads for intercity travel by common carrier.

The years of war and intense development of weaponry had brought great technological advances that could be transferred to civilian production. But even more important was the concept of planned and intensive technological achievement through the deliberate investment of large-scale research and development funds. By the later 1950s the federal government and major private corporations were investing some $15,000,000,000 a year in research and development. The result was an outpouring of physical production that rapidly raised most of the American society to a new level of affluence.

Though this productivity greatly increased the demand for professional and managerial employees, the new technology eliminated millions of other jobs. Improved earth-moving equipment and materials-handling apparatus such as a fork lift displaced laborers and porters. Automation and the use of computers eliminated other whole categories of positions. The skilled elevator installer and maintenance man instead of the operator, the airline mechanic instead of the railway track hand, the computer programmer instead of the file clerk—these typified the changes in the occupational structure.

The results were startling. In the one generation between 1940 and 1970 the United States so reorganized its economy that in spite of sharp increases in population and in total output, it needed about 4,000,000 *fewer* men for unskilled and semiskilled work. For two and a half centuries a prime object of public and private policy had been to keep a massive low-wage labor force available for the heavy and relatively unskilled work of the country, in part by blocking their escape from this situation by a denial of education. And within one generation this force had become nearly useless.

The dramatic increases in productivity resulting from science-based technological innovations are usually associated with manufactures, but in fact the most startling of all the increases in the last generation came in agriculture. New machinery and new chemical fertilizers, pesticides, and herbicides were brought into use. Even more important, however, was the shift of acreage and production from family farms, which were social as well as economic units and had many goals besides productive efficiency, to large, highly commercial enterprises, with a total and sophisticated devotion to profit.

Southern agriculture in general and cotton culture in particular experienced these changes with special force because they had lagged so far behind in the prewar decades. The planting, cultivation, and harvesting of wheat, for example, was already almost completely mechanized by the 1930s; but cotton was still grown by men and mules following the methods of a century earlier. Indeed, there had been no important change in the technology of cotton farming since the introduction of the cotton gin at the beginning of the nineteenth century.

There were many reasons for this backwardness. The harvesting of cotton had defied mechanization for decades. It was impossible to reap an entire plant, stalk and all, as in the case of wheat. The bolls grew at varying heights and opened at different times. The lint had to be pulled gently from the open bolls without picking up leaves or trash or staining the fiber. Dozens of machines were tried and failed. There were available in the thirties tractors and attachments that would have mechanized planting and cultivation, but this offered slight advantage so long as a large labor force had to be held together for the harvest. Nor did chronically poor Southern farmers, further impoverished by the Depression, have funds for investment in equipment.

Wartime labor shortages were coupled with pressures to increase production. And they came at a time when the prototypes of successful cotton pickers were at last available and when prosperous farmers had funds to invest. The result was the beginning of a revolution that began to be widely felt by the 1950s. The proportion of the cotton crop mechanically harvested had risen from almost nothing to a quarter by 1955. By that date two-thirds of the California crop, grown on level, irrigated fields by well-capitalized planters with no commitment to an archaic labor system, was machine-picked. The shift from men and mules to machines had proceeded even more rapidly in the simpler stages of cotton growth, and by the mid-fifties a large majority of the nation's cotton was planted by machine and cultivated and weeded by mechanical or chemical means or by the use of flame weeders. The new technology was ill adapted to the small, hilly farms of much of the eastern cotton belt; but the consequence was only to drive those farms from cotton culture and to concentrate it in the Mississippi Delta and in Texas, Arizona, and California. By 1969 the overwhelming majority of American cotton was grown in Mississippi and the states to the west, and most of it was planted, grown, and harvested with mechanical and chemical aids. The result of all these changes was that by the early 1960s it took only one-fifth as much labor to produce a bale of cotton as it had in the immediate pre-war years.

The need for a large, year-round agricultural labor force was sharply reduced. Farm employment in the United States dropped from 8,234,000 in 1940 to 3,950,-000 in 1960 and about 3,000,000 in 1970. About two-thirds of the agricultural work force, or more than 5,000,000 workers, were made useless in a single generation. Though this decline was general, it hit with special force in the South, where mechanization came later. Nearly two-thirds of the decline in farm jobs in the nation as a whole took place in the South. In that region alone more than 3,000,000 workers were dropped from the agricultural labor force between 1940 and 1970. The great majority of these jobs had been held by blacks, who were freed at last from the cotton fields by a kind of emancipation often more brutal than slavery.

Though the economy as a whole was expanding with unprecedented speed during those same decades, its technological upgrading meant that almost all the increase in employment was in jobs requiring education or advanced skills. Of the 17,000,000 new jobs created between 1940 and 1960, fewer than 1,500,000 were unskilled or semiskilled, and a high percentage even of these was for women. When the peasants of Italy and Central and Eastern Europe came by their millions in the decades from 1880 to 1914, they came to cities with roads to be graded, streets to be paved, ditches to be dug, freight to be loaded and unloaded, burdens to be moved, and all by hand. They came too to factories in which simple labor served primitive machines and to mines not yet mechanized. When the blacks came a generation or two later, they came from mechanized farms to automated cities where the laborer's muscle was almost as useless as the ancient skill with mules and hoes or the fingers trained to snap cotton from the boll.

The city he came to was also being radically changed by the automobile and the postwar housing program. The automobile had become a commonplace of American life in the 1920s, but the Depression and then the war had frozen the construction of roads and buildings before it could completely transform urban geography. Cities remained relatively compact aggregations in which rich and poor, executives and workmen all still lived within what had been horse-carriage and streetcar distance of the offices and factories in which they worked. Suburban towns were small—beads strung along the threads of rapid-transit lines and commuter railroads. Between these thin strips stretching out like spokes from the urban center the land remained for the most part open and rural.

The burst of marriages and children that followed the return of millions of men from the wars brought to an explosive point a shortage of housing already made critical by a decade and a half of minimal construction. It was, of course, the poor and especially the black poor who suffered most from this shortage. Not only were they desperately overcrowded; most of them were jammed into houses not fit for any human habitation. In 1950 about one-fifth of all Americans lived in houses without running water or indoor toilets or otherwise dilapidated or deteriorating. More than half of all blacks were compelled to live so. Though as long ago as 1938 the federal government had pledged itself to the construction of low-cost housing for the poor, little had been accomplished. Of the millions of low-cost housing units authorized in various federal acts, only about 190,-000 had actually been constructed by 1950.

But when the federal and state and local governments turned again to the housing problem, it was not the shockingly housed poor or the new migrants to the city that gained attention. It was the millions of middle-class families, newly married or newly parents or newly having the means to buy houses. The federal government guaranteed mortgages, made capital available to savings-and-loan associations, provided subsidies for veterans, and allowed the deduction of mortgage interest and real-estate taxes from taxable income. State governments made similar tax concessions. Local governments eagerly co-operated in opening new areas for residential develop-ment, changing zoning, paving streets, widening high-ways, installing sewer systems, and building schools. The availability of 97,000,000 new automobiles and trucks produced in the years from 1945 to 1960 freed suburban development from dependence on common-carrier lines, and a new suburbia exploded into being around every major city.

The new suburbs were totally white or very nearly so. For a time after the war the official practices of the Federal Housing Agency discouraged the guarantee of mortgages on homes in racially integrated areas. Even after racial covenants were held unenforceable and the FHA instructions withdrawn, the united policies of realtors, developers, banks, and savings-and-loan com-panies maintained the white exclusiveness of the suburbs. But even had blacks been welcomed, few could have afforded to come. The government, like God, helped those who could help themselves; and the billions of dol-lars provided from public funds to subsidize private housing through mortgage guarantees, tax deductions, and the provision of public services to new areas were available only to those who could afford to buy a house. And not only a house but a car—or two cars—as well, for it was nearly impossible to live in the new suburbs, remote from mass transportation, without a car to drive to work and usually another for the wife's use in shop-ping and errand-running.

The social decision to press ahead full speed with middle-class housing was brilliantly successful. Between

1945 and 1960, 21,000,000 new private housing units were completed. Almost all of the millions of middle and upper-class families created after the war were adequately housed, and a high proportion of older families were more pleasantly rehoused in the suburbs.

This enormous burst of effort, however, exhausted the society's financial and physical capacity to provide housing. During the years in which the 21,000,000 units of private housing were built, only 536,000 units of public housing were constructed. And the federal investment of about $800,000,000 in low-cost housing was only a fraction of the subsidy, impossible ever to measure completely, that was given to middle and upper-class housing. Yet the families of the poor grew as rapidly as those of the well-to-do, and their housing problems were doubled and tripled because of the millions of families driven from mines and farms by unemployment and forced to seek refuge and shelter in the cities.

The only means of accommodating them was to make use of the central-city housing vacated by those who moved to the suburbs, including some housing in older suburbs abandoned by those moving to newer areas. The better quality of the vacated housing was occupied by expanding white families of moderate means. The worst urban housing, already physically deteriorated and rat- and insect-infested, was left available for blacks. But there was never nearly enough of it, and hideous overcrowding compounded the squalor of dingy neighborhoods and decaying buildings.

The decision to house or rehouse whites in the suburbs and place the in-migrant blacks in otherwise unused central-city housing had many unlooked-for conse-

quences. One was the collapse of the social structures of
the areas transformed from white to black occupancy.
Churches and synagogues were bereft of their congregations as their members moved to the suburbs. Buildings
and parishes might remain, but they were husks and ill
adapted to the needs of the new neighbors. Many indeed
were Catholic and Jewish, while the incoming blacks
were Protestant; and conservative churches even of the
Protestant faith were unappealing to those with more
fervent religious traditions. Clubs and societies and informal neighborhood groupings disappeared as well. So
rapid was the transformation of neighborhoods that
there was little opportunity to fit new families one by
one into old frameworks. Since the migration was unorganized and individualistic, few social structures came
with the new residents. The ghettos were left in unorganized turmoil with few means of patterning con-
structive behavior or enduring relationships.

The public institutions were inadequate as well. The
oldest school buildings, the most decrepit hospitals, the
worst paved streets were in the declining sections of
cities abandoned to the new residents. Society's resources
were absorbed in the construction of new facilities in the
suburbs, where tax resources and political influence were
concentrated. The physical conditions of the already
poor institutions declined further under the impact of
crowding and social disorganization, and they became
less attractive to competent staff. At a time when extraordinarily imaginative, able, amply supported services
were essential to meeting the unique and urgent needs of
ghetto residents, their quality and support were sharply
eroded.

This combination—the equipping of all but the very poor with private automobiles, the enormous burst of highway construction, and the suburban housing of the white middle and upper class—not only consumed the resources of the country to the exclusion of possible alternative uses; they also led to further changes in economic patterns. Industries were no longer confined to central urban locations that employees could reach by mass transportation or to points with access to rail sidings for the handling of materials. Subject to zoning rules, they were now free to locate throughout suburban areas, receiving and dispatching materials by truck and recruiting employees from those who could drive to work. Suburban locations were especially attractive to electronic and service industries, which were not offensive to neighbors and did not require heavy materials handling. These were also the most rapidly growing industries providing the most attractive job opportunities. The very ease of private automobile transportation led to a decay and abandonment of public transportation even where it existed, and there was little incentive for the establishment of new transit or bus lines to serve the new areas. Blacks who could not afford to own and maintain cars in the city were hopelessly blocked from employment in precisely those types of plants in which opportunities were largest and most promising.

The contrasting development of increasingly black central cities and white suburbs is shown with special vividness in the unpublished staff studies of Baltimore City and the surrounding county made by the United States Commission on Civil Rights, though very similar statements could be made about many other metropolitan areas. The city of Baltimore itself in 1950 had a population of 956,000, of whom 226,000, or 23.8 percent, were black. By 1960 the total population had fallen to 939,000 of whom 369,000, or 39.3 percent, were black. In the 1960s the total population continued to decline, to 895,-000 by the end of the decade, while the present black population is estimated at 420,000, or 40 percent. Clearly the city will soon have a black majority. Within the city, the black population is further concentrated, with 145 census tracts out of 168 being either almost all white or almost all black.

While the city of Baltimore had been getting blacker, the surrounding Baltimore County has been getting whiter. The 18,000 blacks who lived in the county in 1950 had dropped to about 16,500 in 1964 and continued to decline thereafter, while the white population grew by 350,000, or 135 percent, between 1950 and 1970. The percentage of blacks in the county dropped from about 7 percent to about 3 percent. This sorting of the population by race was no accident. The county has built not one single unit of public housing, and it has even refused to file future plans for providing minority-group housing though this has meant forfeiting its opportunity for various federal grants. This has not, however, prevented federal support of private-housing construction through FHA-guaranteed mortgages. In 1969, more than $11,-000,000 of such insurance was provided in the county, though zoning regulations made the purchase of homes, even with guaranteed mortgages, possible only for middle and upper-class families.

While blacks were being pushed into the inner city, employment opportunities were being pulled out. Be-

tween 1955 and 1965, sixty-five industries offering 4,476
jobs moved from the city to the county; only six firms
employing 248 persons moved the other way. Baltimore
City's net loss of manufacturing firms from all causes,
1955–1965, was 338. In the same years the county
gained 125 firms. Between 1948 and 1968 the total number of jobs in Baltimore City rose by 11 percent (black
candidates for jobs increased about 80 percent). There is
no practical common-carrier transportation to take city
blacks to county jobs. Hence it is easy to understand why
even in prosperous 1960 the unemployment rate of blacks
in the city was three times that of whites in the county.

Conditions of life, of course, vary as widely as employment opportunities. Ninety-five percent of all residents of the county are adequately housed, many of them
luxuriously so. Only about half those in the city are
adequately housed, and the number is declining rapidly.
And the adequate city housing is mostly for whites; few
blacks are in housing units the federal government would
consider suitable for use. Free of the necessity of providing social services—$102 per capita in the city as com-
pared with $7.81 in the county—or of providing police
and fire protection to the central-city business area, the
county can afford to spend $100 a pupil more on schools
while levying far lower taxes, providing more parks, and
in general providing amenities of life unavailable to the
central-city residents. Continuing the policies of Spiro
Agnew when he was its chief executive officer, the
county intends to keep it that way.

Educational development in the twenty years following World War II radically furthered the isolation of
the lower classes in American society. The first major—

even revolutionary—change came with the GI Bill of
Rights offering veterans of World War II the opportunity to gain a college education at public expense. This
was adopted as a democratizing measure, one that would
bring a higher education, formerly the privilege of an
elite, within the reach of most Americans who wanted
it. And so it functioned, at least insofar as blurring the
boundaries between middle and upper classes. In the
1930s about one American in eight entered college and
about one in eighteen graduated. By the 1960s the proportion had changed so that almost half entered and one
in about four was graduated.

But while this massive federal support of higher education diminished the distance between the middle and
upper classes, it radically increased the distance between
the middle and lower classes. Generous as was the educational assistance offered, it was useless to the returning GI
who had no preparation for college or whose family
needs demanded his immediate earnings. It was even
more irrelevant to the hundreds of thousands of young
men, largely black, whose level of literacy was so low as
to bar them entrance even to the Army and who hence
never benefited from any of the provisions of the GI
Bill. Like so many of the government's boons—like Social
Security, union protection, and minimum wages, which
benefited only the well-employed; like agricultural programs which aided only the landowning farmer; like
housing subsidies that helped only the homeowner; like
deposit insurance that benefited only the depositor—the
GI educational bills ignored those who most desperately
needed help.

Indeed, the radical change in the pattern of college

attendance worked to the sharp disadvantage of the undereducated. It permitted the more rapid transformation of the economy through the general use of a technology in which the undereducated had a dwindling role to play. Educational criteria increasingly became an essential part of hiring standards, so that the job and promotional opportunities open to those who lacked a college degree or even a high-school diploma became narrower and narrower and less and less rewarding. In the days of Andrew Carnegie and John D. Rockefeller I, Henry Ford and the Wright brothers, even a high-school education was unimportant—needed only by one planning to attend college, and college in turn needed only by those planning to enter the learned professions. But by the 1960s at least high school and preferably college training, and the diploma as evidence of it, were becoming indispensable to almost any but low-paid and futureless employment.

The second sharp change came with the National Defense Education Act of 1958 and the crystallization of attitudes it represented. Federal aid to education, intended primarily to aid poor rural, and especially Southern, states had been often proposed since the Civil War and had been regularly defeated by the opposition of Southern whites who feared the inadequacy of the education of their own children less than they feared an improvement in the education of blacks that might emancipate them from the quasi-serfdom in which they were still held. The stimulus that finally made possible the passage of the 1958 bill came from the shock of the successful Russian orbiting of a satellite in 1957. This startled Americans from their complacent assumption of world technological superiority. And it gave ammunition to those, like Admiral Hyman Rickover, who had long maintained that American education was too largely concerned with and too indulgent of the dull, the ill-prepared, and the unmotivated, and who demanded that it be made more rigorous and redirected to give special care to the gifted and able.

So it was that when general federal aid to elementary and secondary education came at last it was not to aid the basic education of the poor but the more rigorous training of the able in science, mathematics, and modern foreign languages. A similar elitism and demand for rigor caused the university academic community to take a belated interest in secondary education. With foundation and later with federal assistance, the content of secondary (and, where relevant, elementary) education was radically revised, first in physics, then in mathematics, modern languages, and the other sciences. The revised textbooks and teaching methods that came from these studies won quick and general adoption. They were aimed at giving the students a clearer theoretical insight into the subject which improved their preparation for university work. But there was not until the late sixties any comparable attention to problems of basic education in reading and numerical skills; and the more specific orientation of high schools toward college preparation may have made them even less effective in giving less fortunate youths adequate mastery of simple communications skills or vocational training or a better ability to make realistic improvements in their own lives.

The sorting out of students by socio-economic class, with federal subsidy going almost entirely to the upper and middle groups, was carried further as a result, on the one hand, of the intense overcrowding of colleges and universities and, on the other, of the massive programs of support of campus-based research undertaken by the Department of Defense, the National Institutes of Health, the Atomic Energy Commission, the National Aeronautics and Space Administration, the National Science Foundation, and other federal agencies. During the 1930s almost all colleges and universities were hungry for students. For white students at least, admission in those years was easy for anyone who could meet minimal standards and make modest tuition payments. The flood of students pouring into the colleges since 1945 as a result of veterans' legislation, of changing patterns of college attendance, and, since the mid-1960s, of the postwar baby boom, created wholly new problems of college admission. The most desired colleges and universities could take only a very small fraction of qualified applicants. Selection for admission was determined in large part on the basis of written tests of mathematical and verbal skills administered throughout the country on a uniform basis. Success in these tests required extensive prior experience in abstract communication at rather a high level and thorough secondary-school training in verbal and mathematical precision. Relatively few blacks, however gifted and intelligent, had had an opportunity to acquire such experience or training, either at home or at school; and few indeed on the basis of competitive tests could win admission to the more desirable colleges. In academically less rigorous Southern institutions, "desegregated" by court order or pressures of public opinion, hostile social attitudes and threats supplemented competition as a barrier to black enrollment. Few black youths wanted to spend all their college years, traditionally golden years of youth, surrounded by a cold wall of aversion and hostility and on tense and constant guard. As a result, in spite of the official desegregation of higher education, only a very few thousand blacks in the early 1960s were enrolled in good, predominantly white, colleges and universities. In the institutions of highest prestige, the Ivy League schools and comparable Western and Midwestern institutions, and in the principal Southern universities, the enrollment in any given institution could be measured in the few dozens and in all together in the few hundreds. And these few hundreds, with relatively rare exceptions, were children of well-to-do parents who themselves had had better than average educational opportunities. The principal American institutions of higher education, which trained those who took dominant places in the society, were open to those blacks who were white in all but color; but in the mid-sixties they were still playing no part in any serious effort to integrate the mass into American life.

Blacks who went to college at all, as increasing numbers did, were still likely in the mid-sixties to attend "Negro" colleges or relatively low-level community or urban colleges. The contrast between these schools and the best colleges and universities widened sharply in the decade. The official end of segregation relieved the pressure Southern states had felt to bring Negro colleges as rapidly as possible toward equality with white institutions; and private sources of support, idealistically concerned with integration, became reluctant to contribute to black institutions whose existence preserved segregation.

At the same time, federal research grants became a major source of university support, and these grants were channeled to institutions that already had very strong faculties and research facilities. In 1968, 69 percent of federal grants went to 100 of the more than 2,000 colleges and universities in the United States, and in 1963 the top 100 institutions had received 85 percent of all such grants. Blacks made up only a tiny percentage of the enrollment in these privileged schools, most of which made no special effort to seek black students, especially those of lower economic classes, until near the end of the 1960s. The expenditure per student in the elite schools was five to ten times that in the schools serving primarily blacks.

While the integration of black and white students progressed only minimally in colleges and universities, it actually lost ground at the high-school and especially the elementary-school level in the decade following the Brown decision. The Supreme Court's holding was ignored in the deep South and given only token obedience in the upper South; and neither the Eisenhower nor the Kennedy administrations took any realistic steps to enforce it. Only in such border states as Maryland and Kentucky and in the District of Columbia were legally segregated schools systems actually ended; and even in those jurisdictions the rapid removal of white children from central urban schools quickly restored a largely segregated situation. What gains there were elsewhere were more than offset by the increasing racial separation in Northern urban schools. By the late 1960s many of these were more completely segregated than Southern urban systems.

The black community had been interwoven with the white in the earlier South. The very intensity of the policies, both official and unofficial, taken to insure the subordination and discipline of Negroes was a measure of the indispensability of the black labor force to the Southern economy. The separateness of the two communities was compromised by a myriad of specific relations between individual blacks and individual whites: relations of mutual economic dependence, of friendship and hostility, of complex personal knowledge, which bound the two into a whole. However meager the lot, however humiliating the subordination of blacks within that whole, they were bound as an inextricable part of it. They could neither escape it nor be discarded by it.

One reason for the lessening intransigence of the South on civil rights was its declining need to exploit the black labor force. It was increasingly possible for white Southerners to see an economic future for their region not based on a large, black, semiskilled labor force working for bare subsistence income. The urban economy was coming to dominate the South like the rest of the country, and throughout rural areas new modern factories were spread, which provided off-farm employment for an increasing proportion of the rural whites. The shift from crops to cattle and timber and from hand to mechanical and chemical processes of cultivation completed the revolution. Freed from dependence on underpaid black labor, the new managers of the South's economy replaced an anxious concern for the continued exploitation of blacks with a hostile indifference.

The blacks who came to the Northern and Western cities in the postwar decades were pushed by the relentless closing of opportunity in the South rather than pulled, as in the two world wars, by Northern demand for their labor. Unwanted in the cities as well, hundreds of thousands of laborers displaced from the farms experienced in the explosively growing ghettos the corrupting stain of uselessness. As their hands and skills were maladapted to urban employment needs they were themselves maladapted to Northern urban living. They came, struck loose from the rhythmic cycles of plantation labor, from the patterning embrace of family and church and friendship. Riven from the assuring regularities of the only life they had known and placed in helpless confrontation with a new and menacing life, many of the migrant blacks were robbed of the slender confidence and self-esteem that had survived their earlier lives. And the communities themselves into which they moved had little in the way of helpful internal organization by which they could repattern their lives.

The result was a series of atomistic and anarchic communities, in which there was little structure to aid the weak, affirm values and patterns of life, or give a voice to the community's needs. The ghettos became concentrates of social pathology in which unemployment, crime, drug addiction, school failure, random violence, and aimless drifting reached appalling heights. Hundreds of thousands of blacks—indeed the great majority—armed with inconceivable strengths, survived this social chaos to maintain stable homes and find useful jobs. But for other hundreds of thousands the flight from the plantation economy by which they had been discarded became a tragedy of human wreckage. They lived in squalor, with little dignity and less hope, their children numbed and tossed aside by a contemptuous school system and corrupted by the life of the streets.

The gulf between black and white grew wider, perhaps beyond bridging. In the rural South the lives of both races had been intertwined physically and economically, blurring the bleak edges of oppression. But a black in Harlem or Hough or Watts or Woodlawn might go weeks without seeing a white save as an emissary of authority—as a policeman or teacher or welfare worker or landlord's agent—or else as a shopkeeper he regarded as extortionate. Yet the distant white wealth and security was visibly at hand. Residents of Park Avenue slums along the railroad tracks north of 96th Street in New York could look a few blocks south to the city's wealthiest residences, and every night on the television that was the outward window of the poorest homes the country's opulence was unceasingly paraded. That political rhetoric and Congressional act and Supreme Court decision alike endlessly proclaimed the equality of all men made this vast and daily viewed inequality the more bitter to bear.

Once more the benison of most Americans had become the curse of blacks. The continent-wide stretch of nearly free land that had offered dignity and independence and the chance of wealth to all others had been the very cause of black enslavement. The revolution that had declared all men equal had forced a tacit denial of black humanity. The Constitution that guaranteed the rights of white men gave a formal legal sanction to slavery, a sanction immutable save by war. The New Deal protected the home of the homeowner, the deposits of the bank depositor, the right of the securities investor to honest disclosure, the right of the farm owner to minimum prices, the right of the union worker to organize and have his union recognized, the right of employees in industry to social security and a minimum wage. But these New Deal measures did nothing for the man who owned no home or farm, had no money to invest or deposit, was excluded from unions, and worked in agriculture or domestic service—in short, for the black. Indeed though its relief programs mitigated the worst poverty of blacks and whites alike, the total impact of the New Deal was to widen the gap between those with property or a skilled job, which included most whites, and those with neither, which included most blacks, and to give federal recognition and stability to what had been local and private patterns of discrimination.

So it was with the massive investment of the 1950s and 1960s in creating an affluent and well-educated society based on swift technological advance. This dramatic thrust markedly raised the general standard of living of most Americans. It gave them cars and TV sets and dishwashers and air-conditioners and for many of them new homes in the suburbs. It built them new schools and new hospitals, and new, clean, well-lighted, air-conditioned offices and factories in which to work, away from the dirt and noise and congestion of the cities. It did much to broaden access to the privileges of life. A college education became a possibility for half the population instead of for a select few, and skilled blue-collar workmen came to enjoy amenities of life not greatly different from those of the wealthy. The boundaries between upper, middle, and lower-middle classes were sharply reduced.

But these very changes isolated and excluded the poor, and especially the black poor. The more widespread higher education, the more deprived those who lack it.

The more universal the opportunity to earn high pay by the application of advanced skills to sophisticated equipment, the more useless and unemployable are they who lack such skills. The more completely society is equipped with private automobiles, the more mass transportation is neglected and abandoned, and the more isolated and helpless are the poor when high mobility is required to get to a job. The higher the proportion of the population that can be rehoused in new suburban housing, the more the old, central-city residential areas become a neglected and decaying ghetto. As the gap between the middle and upper classes narrowed, the gap between the middle, even the lower-middle, and the lower classes widened to a chasm.

The exclusion from a needed and productive role in society of several million blacks on whose labor major sectors of the economy had formerly depended ravaged the lives of millions of blacks far more than the halting progress in civil rights healed them.

CHAPTER THIRTEEN

In Which Whites are Driven to Find New Uses for Blacks

BLACKS AND WHITES are likely to view the developments of the decade from 1954 to 1964 in radically different ways. Whites see the Brown decision, the subsequent Supreme Court actions voiding discriminatory laws and the civil-rights acts of 1957 and thereafter as having struck down the final legal impediments to full black equality in education, in travel and public accommodation, in employment, and in housing. What more, ask even friendly whites, can blacks want? Public discrimination having been voided by the courts and private discrimination forbidden by statute, blacks are now free to find and win their own place in competitive American life, and the question can be closed.

While whites looked at the legalities, blacks experienced the realities. The reality they experienced was the massive closing off of opportunity for the unskilled and for those whose only skill was farming or mining. It was the recognition that the halfheartedness of Southern resistance to the later civil-rights acts measured not so much growing tolerance and moderation as indifference to a group no longer important enough to the Southern economy to justify the effort to confine them to sub-sistence-rewarded labor. The reality was the mass flight of refugees from farm and mine to urban slum, one of the largest refugee movements in history, involving the uprooting and transplanting of millions of people. Part of the reality was the overt or subtle defiance of law. Supreme Court decision or no, Southern schools re-mained almost totally segregated in an openly organized "massive resistance" for more than a decade after 1954. Realtors and landlords gave only the most formal and perfunctory recognition to open housing laws, and with an occasional token exception white areas remained ex-clusively white and black areas black. Expansion of black housing forced by the migration extended but did not alter the segregated areas. Labor unions found it possible to ignore equal-opportunity legislation, and blacks re-mained, as effectively as before, barred from craft-union jobs. Southern public officials, especially in rural areas, continued their lawless disregard of the Fifteenth Amendment, and until the passage of the Civil Rights Act of 1965 most Southern blacks were still barred from the polls.

But even where the civil-rights acts and decisions were observed, their effect was largely confined to middle and upper-class blacks. Freedom to patronize any hotel or restaurant or theater without embarrassment was a minimal recognition of the human dignity of a Negro lawyer or doctor or businessman; but it meant little to a bewildered and unemployed black refugee from the Mississippi Delta. The care with which Southern blacks, especially rural blacks, had been denied an opportunity for an education that would offer them a vocational escape was proved to have been remarkably effective. In the face of that long and deliberate deprivation, it required only an impartial administration of middle-class-oriented and abstract aptitude tests to screen blacks from college, or of standard recruiting tests to bar them from skilled jobs or even from the armed services, or of normal literacy tests to bar them from the polls, or of traditional zoning ordinances and credit tests to confine blacks to poor and deteriorating residential areas.

As the number of urban blacks, especially in the North and Midwest and on the Pacific Coast, increased with astonishing rapidity in the years from 1950 to 1965, the conditions of life in the Northern core cities rapidly deteriorated. Few bodies of refugees can have been less well adapted to the life to which they fled than the black peasant laborers driven from Southern farms. Illiterate or semiliterate, untrained in factory work, unaccustomed to city ways, long habituated to a repetitive rhythm of life dominated by other men's decisions, timid of self-assertion, they had few skills for survival in the harsh and crowded life of the city. Many were nearly unemployable in urban terms. Bewildered parents were unable to maintain authority over their children and a sort of sour and embittered anarchy came to prevail in many of the ghetto areas. Housing deteriorated rapidly when overcrowded with tenants unused to urban living and when landlords found it only too easy to keep their properties occupied whether or not they maintained them in decent condition. City services became less and less adequate as more demands were placed against a declining tax base.

But the shocking decay of social services in the inner city was due to indifference and hostility as much as to the confrontation between increasing demands and decreasing revenues. The sanitation, police, welfare, and educational systems operating in the black ghettos were almost entirely supervised and largely manned by whites of backgrounds and life-styles radically different from those of most of the blacks with whom they worked. They came largely from lower-middle-class homes and neighborhoods that felt menaced by the expansion of the black population. Their own somewhat insecure self-esteem found reinforcement in a high valuation of their positions in relation to those with whom they worked and of the formal professional paraphernalia of their jobs.

The consequence was visible to anyone who walked or rode through the city streets: the piles of uncollected garbage in Harlem as compared with the relatively clean-kept streets a few blocks south on Park Avenue; the difference in manner of police dealing with ill-dressed blacks in the ghetto and with well-dressed whites in affluent neighborhoods; the contempt and hostility of teachers toward children and parents in black ghettos as compared to the respect, even deference, toward those in upper-middle-class and upper-class neighborhoods.

The reasons for the malfunctioning of social services were institutional as well as personal. The public school system of New York was monstrous in size. Nearly 50,-000 teachers taught, or failed to teach, more than a million children. There were thousands of supervisory, administrative, clerical, and custodial employees alone. The very size of this system kept its leaders remote from children and from learning and required an elaborate formalizing of procedures. When interests, backgrounds, and previous levels of preparation of the student bodies changed, it was very difficult for the bureaucracy to creak slowly into adjustment with the new demands upon it.

By the mid-1960s the white community could no longer ignore the consequences of the expulsion of so many blacks from their traditional place in the economy. No amount of complacence in the "solution" of the race problem through the civil-rights acts and the Supreme Court decisions could ignore the bitter human disaster of the bursting ghettos. A white man might never see this disaster physically, isolated in suburbs or passing swiftly through on commuter trains or controlled-access freeways. But its presence was inescapable in rising welfare costs, in an epidemic of drug addiction, and in a frightening increase in street crime. Public welfare costs in New York City rose from $266,000,000 in 1960 to $1,127,000,-000 by 1968. Comparable increases exploded throughout the country. Federal programs of assistance were designed for the elderly, the disabled, and the dependent child. The federal system simply did not contemplate the possibility that there might be hundreds of thousands, perhaps even millions, of Americans who were neither too young nor too sick nor too old to work and yet who were destitute. The minimal needs of these must be met from state and local funds which were limited in amounts and disbursed with a miserly hand. The exhaustion of local resources and the apparently endless pyramiding of welfare costs forced attention to the unemployed and the underemployed.

In spite of the enormous funds spent on relief, life

remained below the margin of misery for millions of Americans. This had always been true for the majority of Negroes, but the fact had been obscured so long as the poor were diffused throughout a vast farming region, remote from the attention of press and broadcast. The pathology of poverty was not so dramatic when not compressed in the unstable chaos of the ghetto. Books such as Michael Harrington's *The Other America*, television broadcasts on the treatment of migrant workers, Congressional hearings on hunger in America all shamed the public into the reluctant and evasive recognition that a society that they celebrated as incomparably the richest in history, a society that for the first time had brought ease and even affluence to the great middle mass of the people had yet left millions excluded from its bounty, unused, half fed, ill-housed, alienated.

The despair in the ghettos finally broke out in violence in the middle and late sixties—in Newark, Washington, Cleveland, Detroit, Los Angeles, and many smaller cities there were riots of blind and destructive rage. They were not race riots like those of the twenties in which blacks were defending themselves against white assaults—indeed the races came into little conflict. Rioting blacks did not invade white neighborhoods and rarely harmed white civilians. The violence consisted rather of desperate assaults on the conditions of their lives themselves, bursting down the buildings like prisons where they lived, looting the stores that had exploited them, moving destructively across the stage of their misery.

President Johnson appointed an able commission under the chairmanship of Governor Otto Kerner of Illinois to inquire into the causes of these civil disorders. In a remarkably eloquent, percipient, and widely quoted report, the commission attributed the riots to the poisoning effects of racism, which it asserted was dividing the country into two societies, with the black society increasingly cut off from participation and communion with the white society in the management or the rewards of American life. The discarding of millions of blacks from the indispensable if ill-compensated role they had played in the American economy did more to cut them off from the main stream of American life than civil-rights acts and decisions did to integrate them into that stream.

The painful recognition that equality before the law, even if it were to be completely achieved, would not in itself solve the acute social problems of this *de facto* exclusion could no longer be escaped by the mid-1960s. The national mood of contrition that followed President Kennedy's assassination, together with the massive Democratic victory in the 1964 election and President Johnson's vigorous leadership, made it possible to attack the economic and social as well as the legal aspects of the race problem.

In 1964 and 1965, in addition to the major civil-rights acts already described, there were enacted the Economic Opportunity Act of 1964 and the Elementary and Secondary Education Act of 1965. These were based on the conviction that inadequate basic education and related lacks of vocational skills were the principal causes of poverty, white as well as black. Hence the first step toward the long-range elimination not only of economic misery but of the social pathologies of the ghetto and the segregation of racial communities would be to equip the no longer needed unskilled labor force to play a more productive role in the national economy.

A beginning toward this objective had come with the Manpower Training and Reemployment Act of 1962. It was passed originally with the primary purpose of providing retraining for skilled workers thrown out of jobs by automation. As the sixties passed, it became apparent that this was going to be a much less acute problem than had been feared, and it was possible to apply funds to the initial training of new or unskilled workers. Vocational programs in the schools were broadened from the traditional courses to include training in the skills in which job opportunities were expanding. Funds were made available for on-the-job training, in which employers received grants to cover the added expense. This program was modestly successful, and some 700,000 persons had received training by 1968, most of whom found a useful place in the economy.

The Economic Opportunity Act of 1964 was far more ambitious. It was to be, in the flamboyant words of the Johnson administration, a total "war on poverty," which would get at its roots and eradicate it from American life. The central idea of the act was that each city and rural area would devise its own "community action program," to be planned and carried out by agencies in which the poor themselves played an active role. It was thought that the citizens of each locality, and especially those who were themselves suffering poverty, would best know what particular ways of using federal funds would most effectively meet local problems. Perhaps even more important, the responsible participation of the poor would in itself help to restore hope and dignity and commitment.

Though the selection of programs and their relative

emphasis were left primarily to local decision, the act and its national administration did provide a repertoire of assaults on poverty. Some were medical. Aid was given to neighborhood health services aimed at examination and preventive medicine. In a very gingerly way help began to be offered to birth-control clinics. Both these efforts were too small to have any real impact either on the health or the birth rate of most of the poor in the country, but they perhaps served as useful precedents. Day-care centers for small children of working mothers were intended both to increase the employability of the parents and to give an opportunity to help meet the medical and nutritional needs of the children.

By far the most controversial elements in the economic opportunity program were those aimed at increasing the power of the poor. The very participation of the poor in planning and managing community-action programs was feared and resisted by local politicians and most city officials, who saw it as undercutting their own authority and diminishing the power they hoped to gain by granting or withholding at their own discretion the boons of the poverty program.

This concern was heightened by programs that provided legal advice and services to the poor, the more so since many of their complaints were against local governments and welfare agencies for discriminatory treatment. In general, the pressures of local political leaders and the local bar tended to limit the reformist efforts of the legal-aid program and to confine it principally to the day-to-day problems of poor clients with their employers, landlords, and creditors and with stores that had sold them unsatisfactory goods. The largest single category of cases in fact remained those in the area of domestic and family controversy in which the poor were taking action only against each other. The Nixon administration limited this weak legal aid even further by dismissing the head and assistant head of the service in November 1970.

Somewhat similarly, wherever Community Action programs began militantly to organize the poor as a meaningful force, able to affect the outcome of elections and the distribution of power within the community, the opposition of local officials and the caution of national grant-making officers were likely to lead to their curtailment.

The principal efforts of the Economic Opportunity Program were devoted to education and training in order to fit the poor more productively into the economy. These activities were intended to complement the regular school system, which had already been strengthened in its vocational training programs by the 1962 Manpower Act and which would receive a further major increase in support from the Elementary and Secondary Education Act already under consideration. The poverty program aimed at three groups: preschool children who might enter first grade already handicapped by the meagerness of their experience with language and with the behavior patterns expected in school; talented youths of poor families who could benefit from a college education but would not attain it without counseling and financial aid; and unemployed adolescents and young people who lacked the experience and skills to enter the economy productively.

The preschool problem was attacked in a Head Start program, intended at first to operate only during the summer months and to reach children who were preparing to enter school for the first time in the autumn. The children were given medical examinations, and essential health care was ideally, though not always actually, provided. Efforts were made to habituate children and their parents to better diets. But the major part of the program attempted to provide an enriching and preparatory experience like that of nursery school or kindergarten. A special effort was made to give vocabulary and speech training that would ready the children for reading. The program proved to be very popular, and in addition to the half million children receiving training each summer, an additional quarter million were enrolled in nine-month programs. As a result, a high proportion of poor children of preschool age were reached at least briefly by Head Start.

At the other end of the school spectrum an "Upward Bound" program was started to encourage high-school students from poor families to apply for college admission and to prepare them for a successful college career. This usually involved summer school for two successive summers on the campus of a cooperating college with a personal follow-through program under which the college stayed in touch with the student during the intervening school year. About 25,000 students per year have been included.

The most expensive and difficult efforts, and the ones attacking poverty most immediately, were directed at reaching young people both out of school and out of work. Two programs were planned for these. A Neighborhood Youth Corps, funded under the Economic Opportunity Act but administered by the Labor Department, attempts to give teenagers some training and job experience while they live at home. The Job Corps is a more ambitious and controversial program that removes older youths from their homes and their frequently damaging environments and gives them an opportunity for several months' training in a residential center. The training normally includes both basic remedial education in reading and mathematics and the development of specific job skills.

The Job Corps program has been full of problems and controversy. Unlike many training programs which had been able to show a high degree of success by concentrating on the most likely candidates for training, the Job Corps concentrated instead on the most difficult cases: not youths with a good school record who needed only specific vocational training or adult victims of technological unemployment who had been good workers and needed only new skills, but rather school dropouts who not only had no employable skills but had never known the discipline of regular and continuous work. Motivation was low, attention spans limited, discipline a problem. A majority of enrollees dropped out of the corps centers before completing their full training, as they had so often before dropped out of school and out of other demanding situations. Those who completed the training were generally substantially benefited and were usually able to get productive jobs with future opportunities. The course of tens of thousands of lives was changed from almost certain tragedy to one of considerable hope. But the program is very expensive—about $8,000 per trainee per year—Congress views it with disfavor, and communities resent Job Corps centers in their localities.

As a result, the program has never enrolled more than 30,000 to 35,000 trainees a year and has never been able to reach any large proportion of the youths in need of training.

The Economic Opportunity Act was complemented in 1965 by the Elementary and Secondary Education Act. The pressure of sharply rising educational costs against the inelasticity of local real-estate taxes had long ago made apparent the need for major federal support of education. Opposition had come over the years from two sources: Catholics and white Southerners. Catholics opposed federal aid that would be confined to public schools, putting privately supported parochial schools at a further disadvantage; yet they had been unable to persuade Congress, in the face of constitutional difficulties and opposition from other sources, to include church schools in any program of federal aid. White Southerners, though the South would be the principal beneficiary, had always feared and opposed federal aid on the assumption that with it would come federal supervision to upset the calculated inequality of white and black education and to force a level of education for blacks that would make them less available for exploitation. In the face of these two sources of opposition, it had been possible to win federal support only for particular educational programs in which the national interest was distinct. The various vocational-education acts from 1916 onward and the National Defense Education Act of 1958 were examples of the sort of narrowly limited measures for federal support that had been voted.

The attack on poverty gave a national justification for a far more general program of federal aid to education, not restricted as to subject and distributed under a formula which would channel aid to those cities and states in which it was most needed. More than a billion dollars a year was authorized under Title I of the act, to be distributed to states and within each state among school districts on the basis of the number of children of poor families enrolled in school. Poverty was defined in terms of a family income under $2,000, a ceiling later raised to $3,000. Other titles of the act placated Catholic opposition by providing funds for textbooks and library books for all schools, public and private, and for central innovative services available to all school children.

This was a popular program, particularly Title I, providing support for the education of the poor. Appropriations under that title were steadily increased from year to year. All told, by 1970 nearly $6,000,000,000 had been appropriated to aid the education of the children of the poor, and it had been spent primarily in central cities and in the poorer areas of the rural South in which the Negro population was concentrated.

In the five years from 1965 to 1970 well over $10,000,-000,000 had been spent on the poverty program, in special educational grants concentrated in areas of poverty and in related efforts. Billions more had been spent in relief grants, food-stamp programs, and low-cost housing projects. All this had been hailed as a total war on poverty; and measured in dollars at least there was indeed a truly substantial national effort to make useful again the unskilled masses, black and white, for whom the technological economy had no place, and meanwhile to soften the horrors of poverty in which they lived.

And yet, little happened. The welfare programs had

averted starvation, but not a lingering malnutrition that enfeebled the bodies and dulled the minds of hundreds of thousands of children. The housing projects had lifted tens of thousands of families from squalor but had never been large enough or numerous enough to keep pace with the rapid deterioration of slum housing, so that on balance the housing of urban blacks was worse, not better, at the end of the sixties. And such public-housing projects as there were were generally deliberately so placed as to reinforce the concentration of blacks into compressed, segregated neighborhoods. Manpower programs, including the Job Corps, had given a varying measure of vocational training to hundreds of thousands; but even in a decade of great affluence and of wartime demands for manpower, black unemployment remained twice that of white, and among young black men it was desperately high. Indeed, had white unemployment been as high as black, the country would have thought itself not in a boom but in a deep depression demanding urgent government action. Employment in the skilled union trades, the better white-collar occupations, the professions, and executive and administrative areas remained in practice closed to blacks in all but token numbers. The steady shrinking of manufacturing jobs in relation to the population, the absolute decline in unskilled and semiskilled jobs, and the movement of office and factory jobs to suburban and rural areas inaccessible to ghetto residents largely offset the lessening of discrimination in employment.

Slowly, individual black families, with the determination, the endurance, the ability to sustain hardship that had borne them up through centuries of oppression, had taken advantage of the new legal situation and had achieved education, useful employment, decent housing, and financial stability. To black Americans in the aggregate, as to all Americans, the fifties and sixties were a time of prosperity, with steady improvements in material well-being. But even the successful black family fared not nearly so well as their white counterparts. The gulf between the income of the average white family and the average black family was far wider in 1970 than in 1945, and it was widening further.

And for the families that failed, black or white, these affluent decades were a time of increasing misery and despair. No longer useful to the society, excluded from all its benisons, their exile was but marked the more deeply by every step forward of even the modestly successful. More of these families of poverty were white than black, but while one white family in ten bore the burdens of extreme poverty, its weight fell upon one-fourth of all black families. And upon this hard core of deep distress and unbearable social maladjustment the seemingly ambitious programs of the late 1960s had almost no impact.

There were three reasons why this was so. One was simply that of size. The billions of dollars so glibly referred to in press releases were usually billions authorized over a several-year period, rather than the much smaller sums actually spent annually. There was never a year in which expenditures in the "war on poverty" even began to approach expenditures on highway construction or similar undertakings that were truly thought to be important. The war in Vietnam alone consumed many times as high a proportion of our national income as the

Economic Opportunity Program, and indeed its demands were the principal reason for underfunding domestic social programs in general. None of the efforts to deal with poverty was ever in scale with the needs.

Moreover, much of the money ostensibly directed at the elimination of poverty actually went to support normal governmental functions. This was most vividly true in connection with the billions spent under Title I of the Elementary and Secondary Education Act. In the decade before this federal aid became available, the school systems of many core cities were approaching bankruptcy in the face of increases in enrollment, dramatically rising teachers' salaries, and a stable or declining tax base from which enormous demands for welfare, police, and other social services also had to be met. The financial problems of poorer rural school districts were somewhat different in character but almost equally critical. The influx of federal aid after 1965 did more to avert collapse than to improve in any marked way the education of children in ghetto schools. Indeed, its principal effect may have been only to make possible the unchanging continuation of the dismally unsuccessful education already offered. Certainly the act has done far more to alleviate the financial problems of urban school boards than the learning problems of urban school children.

The second reason for failure was time. Three and a half centuries of deliberate effort had gone into creating the social and psychological environment of a Harlem resident of 1970. No single spurt of effort will quickly undo those long decades' doing. To heal that old sickness will require a maximum effort sustained over a long time. To say so is no argument for gradualism, rather a recognition of the desperate need for the quickest possible start and the fastest possible progress on an undertaking so vast. But to turn aside in disillusionment because five years have not yet erased history is to betray a profound misconception of the problem.

The most important reason for the disappointing results of our efforts, however, is that they have been vacillating and ambivalent. It was not so during all the decades when our purpose was to segregate and subordinate blacks as an exploited labor force. Then we were of a single mind and united in our efforts. Churches and schools maintained as well as taught the doctrine of segregation. Employers and unions joined in the flat exclusion of blacks from desirable jobs. None rested on the letter of the law or served the minimum of its demands; public officials were vigilant not only to enforce every detail of the Jim Crow laws but to stretch and twist the law, as in the case of voting rights, in order to exclude equality in every possible way. A sincere private dedication stood behind the effort of public officials, and where the law did not suffice to assure inequality private zeal filled the gap. No one felt that once a literacy test had been decreed to keep blacks from the polls and a Jim Crow law to separate them in public places everything had been done that was necessary and the law could be allowed to enforce itself. There was rather a full awareness of the absolute necessity of a total and integrated effort to maintain inequality. Laws for separate schools, transportation, and public accommodations were coupled with a total barring of blacks from most occupations, a deliberately inferior education, a domineering social relation, and a consistent philosophy of separateness and

inequality unceasingly taught to both races from childhood in the home, by peers, in the schools, in the
churches, and in the press.

In the maintenance of segregation and inequality
whites showed consistency, unity, a joining of public and
private efforts, persistence through the years, and unflag-
ging zeal. And they succeeded.

Now whites can find little use for an unskilled or semiskilled labor force and would prefer blacks to play a
more productive role in the economy, if for no other
reason than to be self-supporting and less of a social
problem. And most whites profess to seek (many do
seek) a just and integrated society in which blacks may
be not only productive and self-supporting but able to
live lives of dignity, freedom, hope, and genuine equality.
But in this reversal of white goals there has been no such
consistency and unity, no such linking of public and
private efforts, no such persistence or zeal.

National and local governments combat rather than
support each other: national laws assert a right to vote;
local officials exercise endless ingenuity to evade them.
Public and private efforts conflict rather than unite: public law and policy demand equal access to public accommodations; many private owners skirt the edge of the
law in discouraging black patronage. Different agencies
of the federal government conflict: equal access to all
kinds of housing is offical federal housing policy, yet the
housing agencies in practice continue to build public
housing in ghettos with an assumption of exclusive black
occupancy and to subsidize the creation of all-white
suburbs. Private institutions are ambivalent and divided.
Where once, in the South at least, black inferiority was

taught uniformly in church, in school, at home, and in the public media, today the church may preach integration but practice segregation; the official dogma of the press may be equality and the subtle teaching of the home racism. The highest levels of government pursue a schizoid policy. The President proclaims his devotion to a just and integrated society while he instructs his Justice Department to argue before the courts for a bussing policy which he knows will have and is intended to have the result of preserving segregated elementary schools.

Not only is there a lack of unity as contrasted with our earlier racial policies; there is a lack of sensitivity. Southerners were once able to sniff afar the egalitarian and "race-mixing" implications of seemingly remote proposals of public policy. The most innocuous bills for federal aid to education were opposed because they might indirectly undermine segregation. Liberal interpretations of the Bible were denounced because they might by implication bring into question the Biblical sanctions for slavery. Books showing black and white rabbits playing together were removed from school libraries lest they implant in children ideas that might later lead to racial intermarriage. One who addressed a black as "Mr." was ostracized so that his example might not suggest, however remotely, mistaken notions of equality.

In contrast those who today profess equality have lost that fine sense of racial implication. A government professedly devoted to the rights of Negroes can drive a freeway through a ghetto area, thinking of it only as a highway project without perceiving any impact on black housing. It can adopt a variety of policies that have the composite result of substituting private automobiles for mass transit without thinking of the implications for black access to jobs. It can adopt tax concessions to spur investment in labor-saving machinery without counter-vailing concessions for the employment of marginal labor without any awareness of relation to black employment. It can move a Bureau of Standards from central Washington to a rural area in Montgomery County totally inaccessible to central-city residents without private automobiles, and do so solely on the basis of cost factors without any awareness of conflict with government plans to increase black employment opportunities. It can, indeed, adopt the whole concourse of interrelated measures that sustains white suburbia without thinking of that as a program to create the two Americas feared by the Kerner Commission.

The drive for racial justice lacks not only the unity and sensitivity that characterized earlier white racism; it lacks its realism as well. Those who were intent on black subordination never accepted the words for the reality. They would never have accepted a situation in which the law prescribed segregation but in fact blacks were permitted to mingle with whites as equals. They understood that what mattered, regardless of what the law said, was that Negroes should not in fact vote, should not in fact have more than an inferior education, should really not be able to get other jobs than the unskilled, semiskilled and domestic work for which it was intended they be used, should be brought up from infancy with a clear conviction of inferiority.

Such clearheaded single-mindedness is missing from the contemporary civil-rights movement. The Brown decision is hailed as a triumph, even though in many areas education is more segregated today than it was in 1954. *De jure* segregation can be attacked and *de facto* segregation upheld, as though it made any difference to the education of the children what was the rationale of their being segregated racially. We can feel content with the passage of open housing laws while continuing to live in all-white suburbs and to observe all-black ghettos. We can feel that equal-opportunity laws are the important thing, undisturbed that they have resulted only in token employment of blacks in desirable occupations. When the criminal laws and police instructions make no distinction in terms between black and white, we ignore the enormous gulf between the law's actual dealings with well-to-do whites and with poor blacks. Winning their victories in the courts and in Congress, few white liberals look so candidly at the *facts* of racial inequality or are half so intent to change that reality as were all white racists to maintain it.

But the greatest difference is in zeal and persistence. The white racists were willing to stop at nothing to achieve their goals in race relations. If it took violence, they were violent. If it took fear, the hooded Klan rode. If it took murder, they murdered under the guise of lynching. To that end they subordinated every other political goal. They were willing to stuff ballots if more formal methods of electoral perversion were insufficient and to filibuster tirelessly and unceasingly to prevent legislative action when they could not control it. If it was the price of their racial goals, white Southerners were prepared to let their region be impoverished economically, held backward educationally, and stultified politically by a one-party system. If they could not maintain inequality within the union, they would destroy the union and go to war. And their persistence never wavered down the decades and generations, even the centuries.

It is not surprising that a few years of ambivalent and halfhearted effort, ignoring the realities and giving but lip service to the goals, has had limited success in undoing the work of three hundred years of such zealous, united, realistic, and untiring devotion. And yet even liberals are beginning already to weary of a task but tepidly half begun and to find reasons to suggest that further white effort is unnecessary and unavailing, even unwise. Legal barriers have all been removed, they point out. Not only have discriminatory laws been repealed or invalidated, but other laws have been passed forbidding even private discrimination. Whatever the law can do, they say, to grant and protect full equality for blacks has been done. Hereafter, it is the diligence and self-restraint of blacks that will determine their place in society and their rewards. From now on, they say, it is up to blacks to solve the rest of the race problem by their own conduct.

From a variety of sources come other arguments that would relieve whites of the responsibility of doing more. Dr. Arthur R. Jensen of the University of California has revived the thesis of a possible congenital inferiority in the average intelligence of blacks as compared with whites (and of whites as compared with Orientals) in a much discussed article, "How Much Can We Boost IQ and Scholastic Achievement?," in the *Harvard Educational Review*. Dr. Jensen's evidence is more impressively assembled and analyzed with far greater sophistication than the subjective impressions that underlay similar racial conclusions in the past. But the vagueness with which one must define "intelligence" and the practical impossibility of separating congenital from environmental factors remain to cast doubt on his conclusions as well, and indeed they have been rejected by most of his colleagues. Even if one were to accept them, however, they do no more than suggest a slight *average* difference, with vastly greater differences among white children and among black children than the average differences between the races. Yet somehow Dr. Jensen's surmises have been used by others to transform the conception that there should be separate educational programs for children who learn slowly (itself open to serious question) into a conception that there should be separate programs for black children. (A comparable view, since there is rather more persuasive evidence of an innate *average* black superiority in athletics, would argue that it is not worthwhile to give white children physical condition training that would prepare them for varsity or professional sports!) And one of the implications the public, if not Dr. Jensen himself, draws from his work is that the educational, and ultimately the employment, problems of blacks are due to their own deficiencies. And hence whites have no responsibility to solve them.

The same conclusion is reached by another route in the writings of so distinguished an urbanologist as Dr. Edward Banfield of Harvard University, and especially in his *The Unheavenly City*. The oversimplification of his views that reaches the public is that the social pathology of the slums is a direct consequence of a lower-class life-style that is unwilling to forgo today's pleasure for tomorrow's good and that lives by choice in disorganized squalor. And moreover that this life-style is beyond the

reach of outside efforts to "do good." Once again it becomes easy to say that the fate of poor blacks (or, for
that matter, poor whites) is what it is because poor blacks
(or poor whites) are what they are and that there is little
that middle or upper-class whites can or should try to do
about it.

All of these strands of thought may have combined in
the conviction of Daniel Patrick Moynihan, then President Nixon's assistant, that the time has come in race
relations for a period of "benign neglect," a sentiment
shared by millions of whites who have persuaded themselves that nothing more can be done by official action
and that any further improvement in the state of blacks
will have to come from the blacks themselves and from
unforced changes in the human heart.

The racists of an earlier day would have been contemptuous of the idea that public and private efforts
could not change race relations, and they would have
been appalled at the thought of leaving such a question
to the slow and unforced working out of human racial
emotions. They were activists who knew that men by
acts of will could determine the realities of race relations.
But the administration, responding to this passive sentiment, has quietly reduced pressure for further major
efforts toward full racial equality. The Supreme Court
has been urged by the Justice Department to approve a
judicial doctrine that will allow racial segregation in
urban schools to continue undisturbed in fact so long as
it is not formally prescribed by law. In spite of some
highly visible negotiations with construction unions to
permit the entry of a few blacks into skilled trades, nothing in fact has been done further to increase opportunities

for black employment. On the contrary, economic measures pursued have had the effect, foreseen and accepted
by the administration, of very substantially increasing
black unemployment. An effort was made, in extending
the Voting Rights Act of 1965, to soften its provisions
in ways that would have reopened the opportunities for
Southern evasive tactics to limit black voting. The administration and local governments acted together not only
to de-emphasize the "war on poverty" and to reduce the
proportion of the federal budget devoted to its programs, but especially to back away from the policy of
giving the poor themselves a major voice in the planning
and administration of the program. The President has
discouraged even the timid efforts of the Housing and
Urban Development Department to facilitate the integration of suburbs. Indeed, the administration has cut itself
off from all but the least militant blacks and from whites
who vigorously champion blacks so that there is no voice
raised in the White House or listened to there that ex-
presses the views or interests of black masses. Indeed, the
principal response of the administration and its allies to
the bitterness and disorder arising from the despair of
blacks and the outrage of their white sympathizers has
been to promise a more vigorous and uninhibited use of
the police and the law to smother its expression.

Save for repeated attacks on "permissiveness," a great
passivity about social problems has in fact characterized
the whole administration program. There has been no
sense of urgency about slums, about unemployment,
about education—no sense of wrongs to be righted.
There has been, on the contrary, a devotion to preserving those patterns of the American society and economy

in which the poor, and particularly the black poor, have the least part. The continued insulation of the white suburban society has remained a tacit but vigorously supported goal.

There can be no doubt that in pursuing this course the administration has reflected the view of a high proportion, probably a majority, of whites. Even liberals have found it expedient to speak softly of their desire to give any further active aid to blacks. The fact that whites now have little need to continue the exploitation of blacks as a subordinated laboring force has not meant that they would welcome them as equals and associates. Far from it. Once the initial withdrawal from systematic subordination was far along, the strong thrust of white society has been to withdraw also from responsibility for or contact with the black community: to move their residences out of the black-invaded central cities; to withdraw their children from schools attended by blacks; to dispense with the use of black servants; to build the new offices and factories in suburbs and in small towns away from black labor. Physical and psychological separation answered to the removal of legal segregation and discrimination and permitted the "benign neglect." Even liberal whites wearied of well-doing and tacitly withdrew from the problem, finding in foreign policy, population control, and ecology opportunities to invest their moral energies without threat to their own privileged positions.

But this white policy was not going to work either. After discarding the evil and outworn relation of whites to blacks as a subordinate but indispensable class, it was simply not possible to walk away and leave the new relation undefined. It could drift into a relation of sullen and bitter apartness, corrupting blacks and whites alike, destroying American cities as viable communities, and bringing a cynical debasement to American ideals and an overlay of nightmare to the American dream. Or the relation could become one of equal integration.

But to achieve this happy outcome would demand of whites a devotion of efforts over a long time, as single-minded, as zealous, as intent as the effort whites had long devoted to black subordination. It would demand, as had that earlier effort, a total union of public and private endeavor—government, church, school, press, and individuals working together, as eager now to unite as then to separate, as intent now to achieve equality and dignity as formerly to deny it, as determined now as then to reach its goals not only in the lawbooks but in the actual lives of blacks and whites.

The nature of that relation would not long drift undetermined. It would answer itself one way or another. And the 1970s opened with that imperative hanging like an ominous cloud from which we turned our eyes in weariness and fear.

Bibliography

THE RECENT OUTPUT of writings about race relations
has been enormous and many earlier works have been brought
back into print. This bibliography attempts to mention only a
few works of special relevance to its subject. Those who seek
more extended lists will find them in the excellent bibliography
in John Hope Franklin, *From Slavery to Freedom* (3rd ed.,
1967), and in such separate bibliographies as Erwin A. Salk, *A
Layman's Guide to Negro History* (2nd ed., 1967), and Erwin
K. Welsch, *The Negro in the United States: A Research Guide*
(1965). The *Journal of Negro History* reviews or lists substantially all current books and articles of scholarly interest on
race relations and itself publishes a high proportion of learned
articles in the field. The *Journal of Negro Education* has a
broader coverage than its title indicates and provides a very
valuable bibliographical service.

There is no single general history of white racial policies as
such, although Jesse Carpenter, *The South as a Conscious Minority, 1789–1861* (1930), W. J. Cash, *The Mind of the South*
(1941), Thomas F. Gossett, *Race: The History of an Idea in
America* (1963), William Sumner Jenkins, *Pro-Slavery Thought
in the Old South* (1935), Claude H. Nolen, *The Negro's Image
in the South: The Anatomy of White Supremacy* (1967), and
Winthrop Jordan's masterly *White over Black* (1968), among
many others, deal with white attitudes. Gordon W. Allport,
The Nature of Prejudice (1954), deals with racial prejudice
among others.

258

BIBLIOGRAPHY

The best general history of blacks in America remains Franklin's *From Slavery to Freedom*. More popular works include Lerone J. Bennett, *Before the Mayflower: A History of the Negro in America, 1619–1966* (rev. ed., 1966), and J. Saunders Redding, *The Lonesome Road: The Story of the Negro's Part in America* (1958).

Melville J. Herskovits, *The Myth of the Negro Past* (1941), remains probably the best single account of African origins, although some of its claims of close cultural connections between black Americans and the African past were probably overstated, at least with regard to North America.

The pioneer scholarly works on slavery in the United States were Ulrich B. Phillips, *American Negro Slavery* (1918) and *Life and Labor in the Old South* (1929), both written from the point of view of a descendant of planters. His works were vigorously attacked by later "revisionists," such as Kenneth B. Stampp, whose *The Peculiar Institution: Slavery in the Ante-Bellum South* (1956) is the best recent study. Phillips' methods and insights, though hardly his indulgence of slavery, have been defended in Eugene Genovese's brilliant essay, based on Marxist interpretation, *The Political Economy of Slavery* (1965). Stanley Elkins, in *Slavery: A Problem in Institutional and Intellectual Life* (1959), has provided interesting comparisons between slavery in the United States and in Latin America as well as stimulating psychological insights. Lewis C. Gray, *History of Agriculture in the Southern United States to 1860* (1933), presents a masterly account of the economic context in which slavery existed.

Special studies have been done on slavery in a number of individual states. These include: James B. Sellers, *Slavery in Alabama* (1950), J. Winston Coleman, *Slavery Times in Kentucky* (1940), Charles Sackett Sydnor, *Slavery in Mississippi* (1933), and Chase Mooney, *Slavery in Tennessee* (1957). Richard C. Wade, *Slavery in the Cities: the South, 1820–1860* (1964), treats an often neglected aspect.

Free Negroes in the antebellum period are treated in Leon Litwack, *North of Slavery: The Negro in the Free States, 1790–1860* (1961), and in a number of monographs and articles on individual states listed in the bibliographies noted above.

The problem of slavery and equality presented by the Revolution, the Declaration of Independence, and the Constitution receive at least some attention in the standard histories of the Revolutionary period. Benjamin Quarles, *The Negro in the American Revolution* (1961), is stronger on black contributions than on white policy and ideology, which are better treated in Jordan, *White over Black,* cited above.

The rise of antislavery sentiment is treated in Alice Tyler, *Freedom's Ferment: Phases of American Social History to 1860* (1944), which places abolitionism in the context of other liberal movements, Gilbert H. Barnes, *The Anti-Slavery Impulse, 1830–1844* (1933), and the more recent Louis Filler, *The Crusade Against Slavery, 1830–1860* (1960), and Dwight L. Dumond, *Anti-Slavery: The Crusade for Freedom in America* (1961).

Most of the enormous literature on the Civil War and its causes touches upon slavery and white racial policy at least indirectly; John Hope Franklin, *The Emancipation Proclamation* (1963), is especially important.

Reconstruction, following the Civil War, brought the first comprehensive and deliberate effort to construct a new racial policy, which has been treated in an abundant literature. The period was first extensively studied in the early 1900s, when imperialism and the need to deal with an influx of alien immigrants had led Northern writers to take a newly sympathetic attitude toward Southern efforts to sustain a traditional society against the intrusion of "lesser" races. This view was best expressed by W. A. Dunning in his *Reconstruction, Political and Economic* (1907). A number of Dunning's students wrote monographs on Reconstruction in individual states, listed in the bibliographies previously cited. Although this point of view has not disappeared, most recent histories of the period have been sympathetic to the efforts of blacks and Northern radicals. Kenneth Stampp, *The Era of Reconstruction* (1965), is one of the best of the "revisionist" studies. Others include John Hope Franklin, *Reconstruction after the Civil War* (1961), and Rembert W. Patrick, *The Reconstruction of the Nation* (1967). A number of works have revised earlier views of the Reconstruction in individual states. Among the best of these are Vernon L. Wharton, *The Negro in Mississippi, 1865–1890* (1947), and Joel Williamson, *After Slavery, The Negro in South Carolina During Reconstruction* (1965). Special topics are treated in James M. McPherson's important *The Struggle for Equality: Abolitionists and the Negro in the Civil War and Reconstruction*

(1964), Joseph D. James, *The Framing of the Fourteenth Amendment* (1956), William Gillette, *The Right to Vote: Politics and the Passage of the Fifteenth Amendment* (1965), and George R. Bentley, *A History of the Freedmen's Bureau* (1955).

The period from the Reconstruction to World War I is treated in three important works of Vann Woodward: *Reunion and Reaction: The Compromise of 1877 and the End of Reconstruction* (1951), *Origins of the New South, 1877–1913* (1951), and *The Strange Career of Jim Crow* (2nd rev. ed., 1966). Another major work is Rayford W. Logan, *The Negro in American Life and Thought: The Nadir, 1877–1901* (1954). Paul H. Buck, *The Road to Reunion, 1865–1900* (1937), deals with the general background. Paul Lewinson, *Race, Class and Party: A History of Negro Suffrage and White Politics in the South* (1932), deals with disenfranchisement. Ray Stannard Baker, *Following the Color Line,* a collection of vivid magazine articles originally published in 1908, has been reissued as a paperback.

The northward and cityward migration of Southern rural blacks is treated in Emmett J. Scott, *Negro Migration during the War* (1920), Chicago Commission on Race Relations, *The Negro in Chicago: A Study of Race Relations and a Race Riot* (1922), Louise V. Kennedy, *The Negro Peasant Turns Cityward* (1930), James W. Johnson, *Black Manhattan* (1930), and Clyde Vernon Kiser, *Sea Island to City: A Study of St. Helena Islanders in Harlem and Other Urban Centers* (1932).

During the 1930s a new interest developed among sociologists and anthropologists in blacks and race relations, centering largely in the University of Chicago and the Institute for Research in Social Science of the University of North Carolina. Among the products of this movement were: Allison Davis and John Dollard, *Children of Bondage: The Personality Development of Negro Youth in the American South* (1940), Allison Davis, Burleigh B. Gardner and Mary R. Gardner, *Deep South: A Social Anthropological Study of Caste and Class* (1941), Howard W. Odum, *Southern Regions of the United States* (1936), Hortense Powdermaker, *After Freedom: A Cultural Study in the Deep South* (1939), Arthur F. Raper, *The Tragedy of Lynching* (1933), and *Preface to Peasantry: A Tale of Two Black Belt Counties* (1936), Rupert B. Vance, *Human Factors in Cotton Culture* (1929), *Human Geography of the*

The White Use of Blacks in America

South (1932), and *All These People: The Nation's Human Resources in the South* (1945).

There is no satisfactory single history of the New Deal's relations to Negroes, but the standard histories of the Roosevelt era and the various New Deal agencies all touch the problem. Bernard Sternsher, ed., *The Negro in Depression and War: Prelude to Revolution, 1930–1945* (1969), brings together an important collection of journal articles. Herbert Garfinkel, *When Negroes March* (1959), describes the 1941 "March on Washington," the threat of which led to the first Fair Employment Practices Committee. Malcolm H. Ross, *All Manner of Men* (1948), describes its subsequent history. Ulysses Lee, *U.S. Army in World War II: The Employment of Negro Troops* (1966), is an official history; Walter White, *Rising Wind* (1945), is an unofficial one.

The literature on post-World War II developments is overwhelming and only highlights can be listed. Gunnar Myrdal, *An American Dilemma: The Negro Problem and American Democracy*, 2 vols. (1943), was a landmark study that laid the foundation for most of the writing on the subject in the following decades. Numerous paperback anthologies of original sources and journal articles regularly appear and add to the bodies of material available. Notable among these are August Meier and Elliott Rudwick, eds., *The Making of Black America*, 2 vols. (1969), Earl Raab, ed., *American Race Relations Today: Studies of the Problems Beyond Desegregation* (1962), and Charles E. Wynes, ed., *The Negro in the South Since 1865: Selected Essays in American Negro History* (1965). Talcott Parsons and Kenneth Clark, eds., *The Negro American* (1966), is an important symposium.

A convenient summary of legal developments is Morroe Berger, *Equality by Statute: The Revolution in Civil Rights* (rev. ed., 1967). All civil-rights acts, from 1875 to 1968, are given in full, with excerpts from relevant Presidential messages, Congressional committee reports and debates, earlier versions of the bills, and Supreme Court decisions and opinions, in Bernard Schwartz, ed., *Statutory History of the United States: Civil Rights*, 2 vols. (1970).

The reports of the President's Committee on Civil Rights appointed by President Truman and the subsequent statutory Civil Rights Commission are important, especially the former's

To Secure these Rights (1947), and the latter's *Freedom to the Free: A Century of Emancipation, 1863-1963* (1963), written for the Commission by John Hope Franklin.

Eli Ginzberg and Alfred S. Eichner, *The Troublesome Presence: American Democracy and the Negro* (1964), is a useful study of white political policies.

Louis R. Harlan, *Separate and Unequal* (1958), studies Negro education in the South during that region's educational revival, from 1900 to 1915. Henry Allen Bullock, *A History of Negro Education in the South from 1619 to the Present* (1967), is a good general history. Innumerable specialized accounts and studies of problems have followed the 1954 Supreme Court decision outlawing segregated schools. One of the best is Benjamin Muse, *Ten Years of Prelude: The Story of Integration since the Supreme Court's 1954 Decision* (1964).

Arnold M. Rose, ed., *The Negro Protest* (*Annals of the American Academy of Political and Social Science*, Vol. 357, 1965), is a convenient summary of black movements, both nonviolent and militant.

James H. Street, *The New Revolution in the Cotton Economy* (1957), explains the technological developments that spurred the black exodus from Southern farms.

Among the many recent studies of the economy that have special relevance to the problems of blacks are: Kenneth Clark and Jeannette Hopkins, *A Relevant War Against Poverty* (1968), Eli Ginzberg, *Manpower Agenda for America* (1968), Michael Harrington, *The Other America: Poverty in the United States* (1962), Sar A. Levitan, *The Great Society's Poor Law: A New Approach to Poverty* (1969), and *Programs in Aid of the Poor for the 1970's* (1969), and James H. Scoville, *The Job Content of the American Economy* (1969).

A few of the many recent studies of race problems that are especially relevant are: Margaret J. Butcher, *The Negro in American Culture* (1956), Leonard Broom and Norval D. Glenn, *Transformation of the Negro American* (1965), Kenneth Clark, *Dark Ghetto: Dilemmas of Social Power* (1965), E. Franklin Frazier, *Black Bourgeoisie* (1957), Eli Ginzberg, *The Negro Potential* (1962), Nat Hentoff, *The New Equality* (1964), Louis L. Knowles and Kenneth Prewitt, eds., *Institutional Racism in America* (1969), Benjamin Muse, *The American Negro Revolution: From Nonviolence to Black Power*

The White Use of Blacks in America

(1968), Thomas F. Pettigrew, *A Profile of the Negro American* (1964), and *Racially Separate or Together* (1971), Charles Silberman, *Crisis in Black and White* (1964), and Whitney Young, *Beyond Racism* (1969).

Index

265

Index

INDEX

Haiti, 50
Hampton Institute, 102, 103
Hannah, John, 196
Harlan, John M., 189
Harlan, Louis R., 122
Harlem (ghetto), 147, 158–159,
    227, 233, 246
Harrington, Michael, 235
Harvard Educational Review,
    252–253
Hayes, Rutherford B., 95–96
Head Start program, 239–240
Hellman, Lillian, 169
Hoover, Herbert, 163
Hopkins, Samuel, 30
Hough (ghetto), 227, 235
Housing, 146–147, 211–218
    central-city deterioration, 214–
        216, 232–233
        compared to white suburb
        (Baltimore study),
        216–218
    city squalor, 214, 226, 244
    dilapidated facilities, 212
    federal aid to, 212, 214
    gulf between races and, 225–
        229
    low-cost units, 212, 214
    neighborhood transformation,
        214–215
    New Deal, 164
    overcrowded conditions, 212
    segregation, 155, 164
        end of, 188, 193, 201, 202–203
    suburban development, 213–
        218
        consequences of, 214–218
    Supreme Court and, 183, 188
    tax concessions, 213
    veteran subsidies, 212–213
    zoning regulations, 146–147,
        213, 216, 217, 232
"How Much Can We Boost IQ
    and Scholastic Achieve-
    ment?" (Jensen), 252–253
Hughes, Langston, 161

Immigration, 99–100, 113, 139
    employment and, 211

Imperialism, 113–114
Inca Indians, 11
Indentured servitude, 14–16, 19,
    36
Indian wars, 149
Indians, 11, 36, 149, 202
    slavery, 25
Institute for Research in Social
    Science, 169
Interstate Commerce Commis-
    sion, 189

Jackson, Andrew, 59
Jefferson, Thomas, 10, 26, 49, 59,
    65
Jensen, Dr. Arthur R., 252–253
Jim Crow laws, *see* Segregation
Job Corps, 6, 241–242, 244
Johnson, Andrew, 74, 77
Johnson, James Weldon, 161
Johnson, Lyndon B., 198, 235–236
Jordan, Winthrop, 29, 30

Kansas-Nebraska Act, 63
Kennedy, John F., 198, 236
Kerner, Otto, 235–236
Knights of the White Camellia,
    93
Korean War, 184, 185, 206
Ku Klux Klan, 93, 251

Labor Relations Act, 167
Labor unions, 170–171, 228
    and black migration to North,
        143–144, 147–148, 155, 157
    Civil Rights Act (1964) and,
        199
    construction jobs, 179
    equal-opportunity legislation,
        231
    strike-breakers and, 143–144,
        154, 155, 175
Legal advice (to the poor), 238
Lewinson, Paul, 112
Liberator, The (newspaper), 54
Lincoln, Abraham, 10, 32, 49, 65–
    69, 74, 84
Lincoln College, 152
Lincoln-Douglas debates, 49

Index

Public service occupations, 148–149

Public transportation, decay of, 216

Puritans, 25

Quakers, 27, 28

Quartermaster Corps, 150

Race, Class, and Party (Lewinson), 112

Race riots, 154
  pre-World War I, 132

Racial code of etiquette, 128–131
  Southern womanhood and, 130, 133

Railroads
  black labor force, 144
  expansion of, 57–58, 62
  growth of (1876–1890), 101

Randolph, A. Philip, 177

Reconstruction, 5, 74–97, 114, 134
  Black Codes, 75–79, 89
  Carpetbaggers, 82
  constitutions, 81–83, 87–88
  education, 82, 83–84, 85–87, 102
  end of, 96–97, 100, 101
  Johnson and, 74, 77, 84
  religion and, 85–86
  Scalawags, 82
  terrorism, 93–94

Religion
  emergence of Negro churches, 103
  Reconstruction and, 85–86
  slavery and, 25, 27, 42–43, 45–46, 51–52, 59, 61

Republican party, 60, 65, 68, 69, 79, 88, 104, 105–106, 110, 163, 168, 182, 183
  Carpetbaggers, 82
  fusion with Populists, 106

Rickover, Admiral Hyman, 221

Rockefeller, John D., 220

Rolfe, John, 12

Roman Catholic Church, 25, 27, 242, 243

Roman law, 19–20

Roosevelt, Franklin D., 164, 168, 169, 177–178, 179, 182

Roosevelt, Mrs. Franklin D., 168–169

Roosevelt, Theodore, 113, 114

Root, Elihu, 114

Russell, Richard, 194–195

Scalawags, 82

Schurz, Carl, 77–78

Scottsboro case, 172

Segregation, 8, 87, 102, 115–138, 171, 173
  advantage of, 137–138
  armed forces, 150, 176, 180–181, 183–184
  black leaders and, 135–136
  code of etiquette (South), 128–131
  Constitution and, 173, 186
  in education, 116, 117–124, 132, 247
    busing policy, 249
    end of, 187, 188–189, 190–191, 199–200
    Northern urban schools (1960s), 224
  employment, 116, 125–127, 132, 156, 163, 199, 201, 247
  end of legal support, 185–205
    Civil Rights Acts (1957–1968), 194–203
    Justice Department enforcement of, 195, 198–199, 201
    Southern opposition to, 191–193, 196
    voter rights and, 187, 191–192, 195, 196–197, 198, 200–201
  enforcement of, 124–125, 128
  extralegal enforcement of, 128–131
  forms of address, 128–129
  housing, 155, 164, 188, 193, 201, 202–203
  and labor supply, 136–137
  legal structure, 116–117, 128
  and Northern social exclusion, 153
  pre-World War I, 115–138
  in public accommodations, 116,

271

Index

Index

Catalog

If you are interested in a list of fine Paperback
books, covering a wide range of subjects
and interests, send your name and address,
requesting your free catalog, to:

create

McGraw-Hill Paperbacks
1221 Avenue of Americas
New York, N.Y. 10020